The First Teacher

Teaching With Confidence
(K-8)

Karen A. Bosch
Katharine C. Kersey

62276

NEA Professional Library
National Education Association
Washington, D.C.

Printing History
First Printing: October 1994
Second Printing: September 1995

Note: The opinions expressed in this publication do not necessarily represent the policy or position of the National Education Association. Materials published by the NEA Professional Library are intended to be discussion documents for educators who are concerned with specialized interests of the profession.

This book is printed on acid-free paper

This book is printed with soy ink.

Library of Congress Cataloging-in-Publication Data

Bosch, Karen A.
    The first year teacher : teaching with confidence / Karen A. Bosch and Katharine C. Kersey.
    p. cm.
    "An NEA Professional Library publication."
    Includes bibliographical references.
    ISBN 0-8106-1862-1 (alk. paper)
    1. First year teachers—Handbooks, manuals, etc. 2. Classroom management—Handbooks, manuals, etc. 3. Elementary school teaching—Handbooks, manuals, etc. I. Kersey, Katharine C., 1935-. II. Title. LB2844.1.N4B67 1994
    371.1'0023—dc20

94-31660
CIP

CONTENTS

Bibliography

Advisory Panel

Melissa Earnest
Social Studies Teacher
Caldwell County Middle School
Princeton, Kentucky

Alicia Alves Mayne
Graduate Student
Special Education Program
University of California
Santa Barbara, California

Richard F. Wong
Graduate Student
Music
California State University
Hayward, California

PREFACE

This book introduces the reader to a range of topics that first-year teachers have identified as issues needing to be addressed. We have prioritized these topics and presented them sequentially for the beginning teacher. The book's five chapters address the identified needs and concerns of the first-year teacher. The book starts with how to begin the year and finishes with how to end the year. We wish all teachers the best teaching years ever!

This book is designed to be a practical, hands-on guide for the first-year teacher. It provides a self-help format that suggests rather than directs, creates feelings of competency rather than inadequacy, and instills confidence rather than insecurity.

The text is precise and was developed for teachers by teachers to help meet the challenges of the first year. It presents data collected by the authors from preservice teachers, first-year teachers, second- and third-year teachers, and veteran teachers who have taught between five and ten years. Data were collected in many different ways: surveys, interviews, observations, discussions, reflective teaching exercises, journal writing, and field-based testing of text.

Definitions

By "first-year teacher," the authors are referring to one who is:

✔ new to the profession.
✔ returning to the profession.
✔ new to a school district.
✔ changing grade levels.
✔ changing from elementary or secondary to middle school level.
✔ noncertified.
✔ graduate of an alternative teacher preparation program.

In addition, the text can be used in the following ways:

✔ Instruction—The text can be used to prepare education majors for the classroom and for clinical experiences.
✔ Remediation—The text provides guidelines to becoming a more effective classroom manager.
✔ Assistance—The text can guide the efforts of the mentor and mentee programs.
✔ Support—The text can assist administrators in planning inservices and special programs for beginning teachers.
✔ Guidance—The text can standardize the management procedures at grade level and/or school level.
✔ Resource—The text provides directions and lesson plans for accomplishing goals in any learning situation.

Main Features

The book has several features that make it unique in responding to the challenges of the first year of teaching:

1. The contents of this book are researched-based. Bosch (1991) conducted a study using a survey designed to identify the problems, concerns, needs, and feelings of first-year teachers. The survey was sent to 200 first-year teachers in Southeastern Virginia. The survey was composed of multiple-choice, rank-order, and open-ended questions. On the returned surveys, many of the teachers described their situations in detail; some even stapled additional pages to more fully explain the first year's trials and tribulations.

    In addition to this study, several groups of preservice teachers, first-year teachers, second- and third-year teachers, and veteran teachers were formed to gather more information about the needs of first-year teachers. Also, six first-year teachers were asked to keep journals to be used as data for this book. Their journal entries are interspersed throughout the book.

    The authors randomly chose twenty-five first-year teachers from the students who had been hired in the area for the 1991-92 school year to field-test the 30-day management plan (see Chapter 2). The twenty-five first-year teachers, kindergarten through eighth grade, met with the authors several times throughout their first year to strengthen the plan and provide us with a fresh look at the problems, needs, concerns, and feelings of a first-year teacher. Ten more first-year teachers were selected the following year, school year 1992-93, to field-test the revised 30-day management plan and provide the authors with more feedback.

The authors feel privileged to have been given the opportunity to get not only into the minds of first-year teachers but into their hearts as well. Thus, this book and its contents were generated by teachers, most of whom were first-year teachers, specifically to help prepare others for the first-year of their teaching career. The authors are indebted to the commitment of these professionals for this material.

2. The emphasis for the book is on teacher preparation for the first year. The book offers suggestions, ideas, and advice from practitioners and experts in the field. It provides lesson plans for accomplishing teaching goals. It relates journal entries and experiences that only a first-year teacher could know, which enables readers to identify with other first-year teachers and with the book's contents. The content is relevant, meaningful, and useful, helping beginning teachers by addressing their fears and frustrations, answering their questions, and giving them hope. It takes the teacher through the first year from the beginning to the end of the year.

   A teacher who was recently hired to begin her first year reviewed the manuscript and said, "I am reading what I want and need to know. I can't just be sent out there without a set of directions."

3. The 30-day management plan provides a framework that first-year teachers can follow. For some, it can be a checklist of activities to develop concepts and goals through a planned, developmental approach. For others, it can be a map to follow to help them feel less lonely and inexperienced.

4. The book serves as a support for first-year teachers in their transition from campus to classroom. It is also for those people who are returning to the classroom after an extended period of time or who might need a fresh beginning for a new school year. It is our hope that this book will meet your needs and support you in becoming a successful teacher. We extend good luck to all beginning teachers.

Organization

The general theme for the book is PREPARATION. The book introduces the reader to a range of topics that were identified as needed by first-year teachers. The five chapters address the concerns reported by first-year teachers: What do I do first? How do I get started? How do I work with parents? How can I save time? and How do I end the year?

Acknowledgments

We would like to express our appreciation to several people who have given much time and energy to this project: Diane Morgan, Billie French, Susan Anderson, K.C. Joachim, Nancy Peterson, and Sheryl Spence.

The authors are indebted to the many students who assisted with survey distribution, kept journals, field-tested the 30-day management plan, and shared ideas and suggestions in many different forums.

We also want to offer thanks to Timothy Crawford, General Manager, NEA Professional Library, and Karen Zauber, editor, for believing in us and our efforts.

CHAPTER 1:

WHAT DO I DO FIRST?

I. THE APPLICATION PROCESS

The graduate faces many challenges in beginning a teaching career, and he or she must start the job search as early as possible.

The first step to getting a job is to fill out applications. Call the school systems and ask to have applications sent to you or go and pick up the application forms in person. Make a copy of the original forms and prepare a rough draft on the copy of the forms. Transfer the information to the original application and mail or deliver it in person.

Choose your references carefully. Contact them to get their permission and discuss your future plans. After the applications are in the mail, your next step is to do some homework. Begin by purchasing a packet of file folders to help you get organized.

SET UP A CREDENTIAL FILE

First create a credential file. Collect the following items:

1. transcript(s)
2. a 2-page resume
3. names and addresses of possible employers/teachers/friends who might be good references
4. letters of recommendation

5. a list of work experiences
6. a detailed description of a few specific related experiences
7. a list of achievements, awards, and extracurricular activities
8. a philosophy statement
9. a sample lesson plan
10. a teaching videotape

SET UP A SCHOOL SYSTEM FILE

You need to be informed about the school systems to which you are applying. Start by contacting someone who is presently teaching or working within the school system. Take notes as this information may be useful during the interview process. Some of the following questions may be helpful:

1. What do you like about this school system or the school to which you are assigned?
2. If you could change one thing about your job, what would it be?
3. Do you feel that your school administration is supportive?
4. Would you say your school system was conservative, innovative, or behind the times?
5. I am applying for a position in your school system. Do you have any advice for me?

Next, try to find out the names of people who have also made applications to the same school systems. Contact them and form a "network of job seekers" to aid each other in securing a job. (Later, this could be a supportive network of first-year teachers). Sharing information pertaining to the interview process, questions, and procedures can add a measure of confidence to a scary experience.

Set up a file for each school system to which you have applied. It may contain the following items:

1. copy of application
2. notes from contact persons presently teaching or working in the school system
3. sample interview questions
4. list of network people who are also making application to this school system and their phone numbers

II. PREPARING FOR THE INTERVIEW

When you have an interview date, immediately do more homework. Pick out the appropriate file and review your application responses. Contact the "network people" to gain information and inquire whether or not they have had an interview. If so, ask about the interview process, procedures, and questions. Drive to the school administration building so that you know where it is and how long it takes to get there. Review sample interview questions. Think aloud your responses to these questions. Use some of your education textbooks to recall favorite underlined sentences, key concepts and practices, as well as theorists' names that can be used to add strength to your responses.

Decide on questions you will ask the interviewer(s). Prepare specific information that you will emphasize during your interview, such as recognitions and related meaningful work experiences. Write short paragraphs containing such information. Rehearse speaking the written information. Role-play an interview. As one beginning teacher suggested, "Rehearse in the shower."

Sample interview questions may include the following:

1. Describe your most rewarding teaching experience.
2. If I walked into your classroom during math, what would I see?
3. How would you handle a child who is constantly disrupting the class?
4. How would you manage behavior in your classroom?
5. How would you motivate your students?
6. What are the strengths you bring to teaching?
7. How would you establish communication with parents?
8. How would you provide writing experiences for your students?
9. In your classroom, if there is a child who never completes his or her assignments, what would you do?

The interview date has arrived. Think prepared, feel prepared, and speak prepared. Dress professionally and arrive early. Be enthusiastic, friendly, and polite. Take your credential file and a pad of paper on which to record names and take notes. Sit tall and make eye contact. Take a few seconds to think about each question before you begin the response. If you are not sure of an answer to a question, be honest with the interviewer and then proceed with a possible response or approach. Mention that you would contact or consult with an expert in the field or a practitioner working with this special population for further information and guidance in meeting students' needs. Ask the questions you have prepared for the interviewers.

When the interview is over, ask the interviewer what you can expect to happen next. Inform the interviewer that you will call in a week to find out the status of your application.

If the next step is to be interviewed by the school principal, repeat the same preparation process.

III. I'M HIRED—WHAT'S NEXT?

You have been notified that you have a job. Take a deep breath and say, "Thank you very much. I'm looking forward to the start of my teaching career."

A first-year teacher described these feelings in a journal entry:

> I'm hired! She just told me that I'm hired. I couldn't get my breath, my body was shaking, and then out of me came this weak, meek voice that said, "Thank you." When I hung up the phone, I shouted, "I am a teacher for real!" Then came thoughts like, Where do I start? What do I do first? Help! Who can help me?"

It may be necessary to make arrangements to return to the school administration building, personnel office, and sign your contract. Now, you must begin your work—to prepare for the first year. You are no longer a student but a teacher. Studies of the beginning years of teaching have described the transition from student to teacher as difficult for many first-year teachers (Smith 1993, Kane 1991, Sachar 1991, Knowles 1990, Huling-Austin, Odell, Ishler, Kay, and Edelfelt 1989; Brooks 1985; Ryan 1970). The following journal entry provides some insight into feeling unprepared.

> My first day, I never felt ready for the kids. I was doing so well before they arrived. I needed more days to prepare. Is this a natural feeling?

IV. BEFORE SCHOOL STARTS

Planning ahead is essential for the first year of teaching. The most valuable time you have is the time between being hired and the opening day of school. New teachers should engage in extensive planning before school starts (Evertson & Emmer 1982; Clark & Elmore 1979). Too many first-year teachers wait until the first inservice day to get started—only a few days before the doors open for students. These teachers are behind before they have even started. Catching up is difficult for a first-year teacher.

As a first step, count the days you have before reporting to the school. Fill out a schedule or calendar outlining your plan for preparation before school starts.

The following suggestions are from veteran teachers and first-year teachers who commented on what they have done or wished they had done before the school year started.

VISIT THE SCHOOL

Over 80 percent of the surveyed teachers suggested that a new teacher visit the school several times before the scheduled inservice days. The first visit will introduce you to the community, school, and the school's staff. Drive around the area and take a look around. See where the children you are teaching live and play.

When entering the school, greet everyone you see. Allow enough time to talk with the faculty and staff. Listen, ask questions, keep notes, and learn.

Find your assigned room. Locate areas within the school: offices, cafeteria, library, clinic, custodian's room, restrooms, counselor's office, gym, audiovisual equipment room, and computer labs. In addition, find the teachers' lounge, vending machines, ditto machine, and copying machine.

Before leaving, borrow one or two teachers' magazines found in the lounge or library. Read the publications and copy interesting ideas. Read some of the September issues of teaching journals. They usually have good ideas for starting the new year.

On the next visit, attempt to learn some specifics about your school and its philosophy. Ask to see and check out the school policy handbooks. Inquire as to the possibility of previewing the curriculum books and study guides. Read the texts thoroughly and begin to think about ways to teach the topics. Start collecting ideas, materials, and information pertaining to the topics. Having the topics in mind will enable you to find relevant materials in newspapers, magazines, and books, as well as identify activities, places, and resources to support the curriculum.

You may want to search for unusual facts, unique activities, and creative ways to introduce and teach topics. Begin to think about resource speakers, films, and materials to build into the unit of study.

Some questions to ask when you visit the school are the following:

1. Ask to see a progress report form and a report card so that you will be aware of the areas of evaluation. Inquire about the grading scale.
2. Ask for a class roster and a school photograph of members of your class (class book, pictures in cumulative files) to begin associating names with faces.
3. Inquire as to the availability of an overhead projector, maps, a tape recorder, and a computer to have in your room if these items are not currently present. The custodian may be able to help you find a large table or two and some additional chairs to create a learning center.

PREPARE THE ROOM

Advance preparation is the key to a successful first day, first month, and first year. The "smooth functioning of the classrooms of successful managers results from thorough preparation and organization at the beginning of the year" (Good & Brophy 1987, 220). For most first-year teachers, preparing the room is fun and a way to personalize the surroundings.

Research shows that effective teachers create positive learning environments by using management skills to organize time, space, materials, auxiliary personnel, and students (Strother 1985). The first-year teacher can begin by sketching the room and making some decisions about room arrangement. The following suggestions are ways to start creating an attractive room.

1. Arrange desks and prepare a seating chart. Begin by identifying a teaching position in the front of the room. Radiate the students' desks from this teaching position in pairs, rows, or groups of four. Consider using one or two semicircles of desks as a seating arrangement. It is important that all students' faces are visible to you.
2. Put your desk in a location from which you can monitor students at work. The teacher's desk in the back of the room facing students' backs can provide a position from which you can make a quick check for off-task behavior.
3. Put up one or two bulletin boards. Make them colorful, inviting, and interesting. Reserve a space in the room for the students to create a bulletin board sometime during the first month.
4. Plan one or two age-appropriate learning centers.
5. Use the computer in your classroom as part of a learning center or as an

instructional tool. Check the availability of software.

6. Ask the librarian (media person) for trade books that are age-appropriate, interesting, and exciting for the students. Set up a class library.

7. If your room is large enough, you can design a reading corner. This can be done with pillows and/or carpet squares. An elaborate entry to the reading center, such as a tent or an igloo, might be an interesting possibility.

8. Plan a unique way to label your door with your name and room number. It is important to establish an identity.

The following suggestions for starting school have been collected from first-year teachers, second- and third-year teachers, veteran teachers, and from the authors themselves:

✔ Send out postcards to students introducing yourself and highlighting the year (see Figure 1). One teacher reported that she sends out party invitations to her class members inviting them to the classroom.

Figure 1. Postcard to Students

Dear Susan,

I am so excited that you are going to be a part of our third grade class.

We will be doing a lot of fun things this year. You will learn your multiplication tables and how to write in cursive.

Please bring a picture of yourself on the first day.

See you next week.

Sincerely,

Student

100 Student Road

Student, VA 22222

✔ Call parents and/or students. Introduce yourself and let the students know that you are glad they are in your class. Suggest to parents that teaching is a shared responsibility and a partnership leads to success for the student. Try calling parents on three separate evenings (i.e., call 1/3 on Tuesday, 1/3 on Wednesday, and 1/3 on Thursday, or five a night).

✔ Prepare a file folder for each student to collect work samples and document certain behaviors. Set up additional file folders with labels such as the following: "Rainy Days File"—teaching ideas, materials, and projects with materials collected in advance; "Fillers File"—dittos, games, interesting facts, duplicated activities, and ideas for immediate use; "Fun File"—for arts and crafts or experiments requiring materials that are already available in the classroom or collected in advance; "Ideas File"—for ideas clipped from teacher journals and ideas from other teachers; and "Bulletin Board File"—for sketched ideas or ideas clipped from newspapers or journals or from other teachers.

✔ Start a file for substitute teachers in which you will put a schedule (see Figure 2), a seating chart, routines, extra dittos, and a list of several fun activities and games that students enjoy. Your principal may have guidelines for this file.

Figure 2. Sample Class Schedule

Date _____		Teacher _____ Room_____ Grade_____
7:35 7:55	Morning Assignments	Sharpen two pencils. Copy homework assignments in composition books. Math: Spelling:
7:55 8:05	SQUIRT	Sustained Quiet UnInterrupted Reading Time— Read a book of your choice silently.
8:05 8:10	Clerical	Collect library books. Say Pledge of Allegiance. Write down absences on absence list. Take lunch count.
8:15 8:45	Science/ Soc. Studies	
8:45 9:15	Music	Walk them to Room _____ (room number), _____ (teacher's name).
9:15 9:30	Bathroom	Line up boys first, then girls. Use the bathrooms in the back hall.
12:00 12:30	Lunch	Table 7. Line up in this order: Children who are buying milks and snacks, hot lunches, then children with lunch boxes.
12:35 12:50	Recess	Recess helpers should get the equipment. Go out to the bus ramp. Children may play on the blacktop or on playground.

✔ Make a large, colorful display of students' names outside your classroom door. Invite them to begin a new year. One first-year teacher suggested placing tennis shoes (sneakers) on the wall outside the classroom door with each sneaker having a student's name on it. The caption placed above the sneakers read, "Sneaking into Sixth Grade with Ms. Morgan." Another first-year teacher used the theme "Happy New Year!" and placed horns, hats, and streamers on the door and a class roster in the middle.

✔ Make a large attendance chart on which students will be able to record their own attendance each day. Laminate for durability. You will be able to quickly scan chart for attendance information.

✔ Make a large chart or bulletin board to highlight student jobs in the classroom. Laminate it and prepare it in a way that allows you to put up new names every week, every two weeks, or monthly.

✔ Make and laminate a chart of the daily/weekly schedule with blocks of time to record the current schedule. This schedule informs the teacher and students of changes, events, or special classes. A blocked schedule form for distribution to students on a weekly basis may be helpful.

✔ Make extra copies of the class roster and the seating chart. These forms are helpful for the many times you must keep records throughout the school year, for example, recording which students bring in required school forms, permission slips, and homework. Teachers can use the forms to document their own behaviors such as the frequency of choosing students to respond to questions. Copies of the class roster can be given to the room mothers and to students.

✔ Create and duplicate a form that can be attached to students' work requiring parents' signature, comments, and the date.

✔ Ask a teacher in the school to tell you what happens on the first day. Take notes.

✔ Purchase a subscription to a teachers' magazine.

✔ Visit a teachers' store in your area.

✔ Review books that will be read aloud to students at an assigned time or as an extra treat. Commit some to memory.

✔ Make a list of required materials students will need.

Go to the stores early before they run out of basic school supplies. A first-year teacher humorously suggested that a teacher supply list should include: chalk-colored clothes, comfortable shoes, and a large bottle of aspirin to begin the year. More serious suggested items to purchase prior to the start of school are:

- ❏ adhesive notes
- ❏ a calendar
- ❏ a large canvas tote
- ❏ chart paper
- ❏ colored markers
- ❏ colored paper
- ❏ file folders
- ❏ file trays for paper collection
- ❏ a grade book
- ❏ hand lotion

- ❏ index cards
- ❏ letter cutouts

- ❏ masking tape
- ❏ notebook paper
- ❏ paper clips
- ❏ pencils
- ❏ poster board
- ❏ a rubber stamp of your name
- ❏ scissors
- ❏ scotch tape
- ❏ a stapler and staples
- ❏ two-sided sticky tape to attach charts to the chalkboard
- ❏ a timer
- ❏ tissues

You may want to purchase books, a bookcase, or other furniture, and a rug or carpet remnants. Garage sales are one place to collect such items inexpensively.

V. PREPARING FOR THE FIRST DAY

The first day is like a first impression—it has to be good. In the following journal entries, first-year teachers reflected on that first day.

> Today was the first day of my career, I can't believe it. I felt as if I was in a daze. It was neither a bad day nor a great day. It was just kind of there.

> My first day went like this: I started, stopped, was interrupted by announcements, started again, was stopped again, was interrupted by a knock at the door. It was time to switch classes. Chaos ensued! Kids leaving every which way for somewhere. Not knowing students' names, I was helpless to prevail!

Several suggestions for a successful first day include:

1. Prepare a letter to parents outlining goals and objectives for the school year. Pass out the letter at the end of the day.

2. Plan an unique way to introduce yourself to the class. An example might be to come to school with a large duffle bag. Inside the bag are things that tell the students something about you. The bag could contain the following: a tennis racket, beach towel, sunglasses, a novel, a picture of a pet, a bag of potato chips, and a diet soda. The students could later be invited to present such a "bag" that would introduce them to their fellow classmates.

3. Prepare an interest survey to pass out the first day. Information taken from the survey will help you establish positive relationships with your students and help them build strong peer relationships. It can make your teaching more interesting, relevant, and personal. Continue to survey the students throughout the year and use the information to make assignments, form groups, and plan enrichment activities.

4. Write student names or numbers on popsicle sticks or tongue depressors. If you use numbers, assign each student a number. Put all the sticks in a jar. Use the sticks to call on students the first few days. This will help you get to know student names quickly. The sticks can be used throughout the school year to call on people fairly, assign jobs, and line up the students.

5. Prepare some review sheets (not lengthy) from the first few chapters of the subject matter texts. Children enjoy maps and diagrams, word puzzles, and math games. The information gained from this is invaluable for assessing students' knowledge and planning how much time to spend on review.

6. Plan the spelling lesson and activities for the first week. Ideally, words that are associated with other subjects will be used as well.

7. Plan some student work to be completed on the first day. Write a positive comment or two on the assignment. Pass out the work at the end of the day with other items to take home.

8. Prepare a few procedures that will be necessary for the first day: use of bathroom passes, sharpening pencils, taking attendance, turning in class work.

9. Think about the cue you would like to use in your classroom to gain students' attention: a whistle, a clap, lights, a raised hand, a signal, or your moving to the center of the room. Teach the cue and begin using it the first day.

10. Prepare some extra dittos, crossword puzzles, or games.

VI. SURVIVAL ADVICE

How do students see first-year teachers? Interviews were conducted (Bosch 1991) with 25 sixth grade students in a large, urban school. The majority of these sixth graders reported that they could identify first-year teachers by the following characteristics: "inconsistent, lenient, nervous, slow to handle discipline problems, want to be your friend, and they have evaluators in their rooms all the time." When asked if students are hard on first-year teachers, they responded unanimously "Yes." Students agreed that the phrase said most often to inexperienced teachers is, "But, my last year's teachers didn't do it that way." When asked if they had some advice for first-year teachers, several students said that they should handle discipline problems faster. Others suggested that new teachers should stop trying to be their friends.

What advice do teachers have for surviving the first year? We, the authors, asked teachers in college classes that we teach to provide suggestions for survival. We compiled the following list:

- ✔ Get to know the custodian and the secretary well.
- ✔ Choose extra-duty assignments that you want and can handle. Don't be afraid to say "No" to committee involvement or assignments. Use the reply "The first year of my teaching career is enough for me to concentrate on at the moment, but ask me again."
- ✔ Don't correct papers or do lesson planning at faculty meetings.
- ✔ Stay away from the teachers' lounge. It may be a very negative place. Find a quiet spot to recoup.
- ✔ Don't complain, as misery finds too much company.
- ✔ Start class as soon as the bell rings.
- ✔ Plan activities for students who finish their work before others.
- ✔ Anticipate the behavior of children before and after holidays and long weekends, on field trips, and when evaluators come into the room.
- ✔ Figure out what to do about homework.
- ✔ Don't be so hard on yourself. Give yourself a break!
- ✔ Don't give up!

It has been said that teaching is the only profession where the beginner is expected to do what the veteran does and with equal success (Moran 1990; Tonnsen & Patterson 1992). As one new teacher wrote in her journal, "I wish we came with a set of directions."

Many beginning teachers have expressed the need for one more college course or text to prepare future teachers for the transition from campus to classroom. It is our hope that this book will provide the missing link between teacher preparation programs and first-year teaching performance.

CHAPTER 2:

HOW DO I GET STARTED?

I. TEACHER AS A MANAGER

The first day, week, month, you are creating a first impression, and the impression that you must make with the students is that you are in charge and very prepared to take control. Many books and journal articles describe the experiences of first-year teachers (e.g., Drayer 1979; Ryan 1970, 1986; Bullough 1989; Kane 1991; Sachar 1991). However, few sources have specifically addressed the needs of first-year teachers in their leap from the campus to the classroom. The first month is a critical time for the teacher to create a strong, positive first impression. This is the time for you to establish your role in the classroom, get to know your students, and create a positive learning environment. Smith says, "It has become apparent during visits with former undergraduate students who were beginning a teaching career that success during the first month in the classroom was critical to future growth" (1993, 121). Arends reports, "Succeeding in one's first teaching job seems critical to someone who has prepared long and hard for teaching" (1991, 439).

The first-year teacher asks, "WHERE DO I BEGIN?" You begin with a management plan. Let's take a look at the planning that goes into the first month in the classroom.

The first reality that the beginning teacher faces is making lesson plans (see Lesson Plan Format, Figure 3, based on a lesson plan paradigm by Hunter 1989) to keep the students busy for the first day or two—or the first week, if you happen to be one of those unlucky ones whose books are late in arriving. The first week is also filled with interruptions and changes. The second reality is the enormous amount of paperwork that needs to be completed during the first few days of school. Many first-year teachers reported that the paperwork was overwhelming and the priority

Figure 3. Lesson Plan Format

PLANNED LESSONS AND ACTIVITIES

- **Topic**—As desired
- **Opener**—To hook the learner into the lesson. It can include review but still must spark interest to move to the new material.
- **Objectives**—The student will be able to:
  1. identify ...
  2. apply ...

   In writing objectives, use action verbs that are appropriate for the six levels of cognitive objectives from Bloom's (1984) taxonomy.

   The teacher must focus students' attention on the objectives for accountability.
- **Instruction**—Ten to fifteen minutes of lecture and discussion (information-giving) per objective. Divide teaching into parts by objectives.

   Teacher evaluation opportunities within instruction that provide feedback are important in making decisions such as to go on to the next objective or provide more input, examples, or practice.
- **Check for Understanding**—A way for the teacher to collect information on student learning. This can be an oral check by asking a question and then asking how many agree, how many choose a and b responses, or if this sentence contains an adjective, stand up. A quick scan over the class or listening to answers provides the information to move on to new material or to give additional input or to continue with the same material.
- **Guided Practice**—Students work with information independently or in pairs or groups, using cooperative learning activities. The teacher provides guidance, coaching, and feedback. This practice provides information as to whether the student would be able to be successful with the material independently.
- **Closure**—Focus again is on the objectives of the lesson. Have students tell you what they have learned.
- **Independent Practice**—Student practices the material independently and the work is evaluated.
- **Evaluation**—Teacher can formally assess student learning at the end of the lesson by collecting work and grading it. Many opportunities to evaluate informally (without grading) are interspersed throughout this lesson plan. (See the techniques of Check for Understanding and Guided Practice).

it took was astounding. The first week must be set up to respond to the realities of beginning the school year.

Management must begin the year, management must be maintained throughout the year, and management must end the year. A major management task for beginning teachers is to teach the students the rules, consequences, incentives, procedures, and routines of the classroom. You must develop lesson plans that emphasize how you want to operate your class from day to day, manage the students, and teach the curriculum.

You must use techniques that encourage appropriate student behavior such as the "positive ripple effect" and "catch them being good." For example, the following statements signal expected behavior: "Mary, I like the way you have your journal on your desk and are ready to start this activity," and "John, thank you for coming into the room quietly from your bathroom break."

Research conducted by Evertson (1989) suggests that placing emphasis on "solving managerial and organizational problems at the beginning of the year is essential in laying the groundwork for quality learning opportunities for students" (p. 90). Teachers who spend considerable time during the first several weeks of school on classroom management are considered more effective teachers (Evertson & Emmer 1982; Emmer, Evertson and Anderson 1980; Evertson & Anderson 1979). Classroom management begins with teaching rules, defining procedures, establishing consequences, developing incentives, and employing strategies and practices to support this effort.

In addition to developing and teaching rules and procedures, several other areas need attention: creating a positive first impression, establishing a positive climate for learning, developing positive relationships with students, strengthening peer relationships, and forming ways to work with parents. The learning circle includes teachers, students, and parents who know each other, are able to work together, and are willing to learn together.

The classroom management plan must be taught, not just told, to the students. The students must know and feel its importance. They must see that this plan is a democratic approach for the teacher and students to work and learn together. Further, the teacher must review, reinforce, reward, and reteach the management plan as needed, prior to correction, in order to insure success.

In the next section, we present a classroom management plan that we developed to assist the first-year teacher in becoming an effective manager. The management plan includes all of the above items and provides a structure that maintains consistency. The plan is rather detailed and time-consuming initially, but it gradually decreases in intensity, thereby allowing the academics to take priority. The classroom management plan serves as the foundation for teaching curriculum and provides the framework from which the teacher can teach and the students can learn.

Every teacher must teach in a manner that FITS—his or her own personality, beliefs about children and learning, and tolerance level for confusion. Beginning teachers have a lot to learn before they come face-to-face with the students. We, two veteran teachers who have had the opportunity to work with first-year teachers, have become sensitive to their need for HELP, GUIDELINES, and SUGGESTIONS that they can put to use the very FIRST day.

Therefore, we have put together many ideas that have already been tried and proven to work in classrooms of children of all ages, genders, and cultures. It is our hope that you will be able to find what will work for YOU. Feel free to adapt, combine, delete, and add. FIND WHAT WORKS FOR YOU. USE WHAT YOU CAN. ENJOY!

II. FIRST MONTH CLASSROOM MANAGEMENT PLAN

FIRST WEEK

GOAL: TEACH WHAT IS IMPORTANT

Key Teaching Areas:
- ❑ Teach Management Plan.
- ❑ Establish and Teach Routines.
- ❑ Establish and Teach Cues.
- ❑ Model Procedures.
- ❑ Develop and Teach Rules.
- ❑ Develop and Teach Correction Plan.
- ❑ Develop Positive Teacher/Student Relationships.
- ❑ Develop Student Accountability.

Strategies for Success:
- ❑ Provide Get-Acquainted Activities.
- ❑ Use Positive Ripple Effect.
- ❑ Offer Praise, Feedback, and Encouragement.

Reminders for First Day:
- ❑ Introductory letter.
- ❑ Index cards.
- ❑ Student's supply list.
- ❑ Name tags or puzzle pieces.

☐ Orientation folders. ☐ Cue signals—whistle, bell.

Most schools have a four-day work week to begin the school year. This management plan begins with a four-day approach. If you begin with a five-day work week, spread the activities for the four days outlined over the five days.

DAY 1—FIRST IMPRESSION

BEGIN THE DAY: Greet the students at the door, introduce yourself, and ask their names, shake their hands, and tell them how happy you are to have them in your class.

OPENING ACTIVITIES: Direct the students to the bulletin board to obtain their name tags. The students will be wearing their name tags during the first day or days. At the end of each day, they will return the name tags to the bulletin board. The bulletin board could be a tree stating, "You are the apple of my eye" and the name tags shaped like apples, or "Mrs. Jones' Class Tree" and the name tags shaped like leaves. If assigned seating is part of your plan, have students match the number placed on the name tags to the number on the seat that provides a fun activity for sharing names and gives you a seating chart from which to begin your first day.

Another opening activity could be to design name plates similar to personalized license plates. The students are given scrap paper to write down ideas. The name plates may have no more than eight letters. The student chooses one plate idea and is then given colored paper and a magic marker to make the plate. The plate is placed on tag board that is folded at the bottom in order to tape to the front of the desk. The students share why they chose that plate. The teacher makes a name plate, too. The name plates can be placed on a bulletin board entitled, "Licensed to Learn!"

OR

In another activity, the teacher makes a large puzzle and places one student's name on each puzzle piece and cuts the puzzle into the name pieces. (The teacher can make several copies of each puzzle piece to use for other activities.) The student is directed to come into the room and go to the back table to find a puzzle piece with his or her name on it. The student is to find his or her seat—the one that has the same puzzle piece taped to it. When everyone has come into the room, the teacher will give the students approximately ten to fifteen minutes to put the puzzle together on the back table. The teacher will preserve the puzzle and post it in the room for all to see. The teacher will refer to it when people are not working together. Discuss with the students the idea that things work better together than apart ("Two heads are better than one."). The third set of puzzle pieces can be used to call on students randomly when too many hands are raised. The puzzle pieces can be put in a can and drawn out by the teacher or a student.

INTRODUCTION: Introduce yourself to the class. Then write the word *fun* on the board. Begin the activity by saying, "I'm going to give you a minute to think about this question, 'What is fun?' and then I am going to ask for your thoughts." Watch the clock and when the time is up, make eye contact with students and ask for responses. Next say, "I'm going to give you another minute to think about this question, 'Why is it fun?'" After some discussion, have the students summarize the "what and why of fun" and begin sharing your teaching philosophy, which includes fun. Discuss your expectations for a positive year.

GUIDELINES: Discuss the following: lunch money, bus numbers, use of bathroom passes, and when to throw away trash. Require a standard behavior to line up, to walk in the halls, and to eat in the lunchroom. Use a procedure for the required behavior and use the positive ripple effect to support the procedure. For example, say "I like the way Row 1 is ready for the line up. They may go first," "I like the way Jimmy walked to his place in line," and "Kate, you were so quick to get in line. Thanks!"

Use many different selection methods for lining up and for grouping students. One method is to assign a day of the week to each row and on that day that row lines up first. Other methods include lining up by: type of shoes, birthday months, clothing, favorite TV shows, foods, eye color, number of pets, number of brothers and sisters, last year's teachers, and so on.

OPENING TASKS: Let students know the materials needed for class: notebooks, pencils, assignment book, student planner, crayons, scissors, and so on. Pass out a list of needed supplies at the end of the day. For younger students, place names and bus numbers on large cut-out bus posters and put them in the room near the door.

ESTABLISH A CUE: Teach a cue to gain the students' attention. Use this cue from this day forward. Wait for their attention and begin when you have everyone's attention. Tell the students the cues will be used at various times to get everyone's attention quickly and especially when the teacher is ready to begin instruction. Again, support this procedure by looking for the positive. Find the students who are doing the "right" things and praise, reward, and reinforce the behavior you want to continue.

Some interesting and effective cues are as follows:

1. A bell, whistle, or clap.
2. Raising a hand and moving to the front of the room.
3. A symbol, hat, sign language, one word, or group of words. A group of words used by one first-year teacher was "Freeze, Look, and Listen." The students enjoyed the phrase and responded quickly.
4. A stoplight, and the red light means stop, look, and listen; yellow—too noisy, quiet down; and green—great job.
5. A rap that the class composes or a clap sequence to begin class. Teacher starts and all join in as they prepare for class and to focus on the teacher.
6. Teacher begins to recite a poem memorized by the class. Students join in when they are prepared for class and ready to listen.

PLANNED LESSONS AND ACTIVITIES

Use the established cue to gain everyone's attention. Teach the first lesson in your management plan. The lesson is how the student will start the school day. This includes the first classroom rule and the routine procedure to begin the school day.

- **Topic**—Rule 1: Be Prepared for Class
  Discuss and teach your first rule and expectation for the class.
- **Opener**—Plan a short role play. Tell the students that you will be going out of the room and entering again and that you want them to tell you all the things they see that are wrong. Come into the class very unprepared. Be rushing, without materials, upset, can't find your lesson plan book, left the quote for the day at home, the graded papers to be returned to students as promised cannot be found, and hurriedly give the students some work to keep them busy without any instructions or teaching of material.
- **Objectives**—The student will be able to:
  1. identify how to be prepared for class.
  2. resolve situations in which they are unprepared for class.
- **Instruction**—Web the word *Unprepared*. The students identify all the examples of the teacher being unprepared for class. Discuss with students how they have expectations for you and you have expectations for them. Web the words *Be Prepared*. The students discuss how they can be prepared for class. Discuss teacher expectations for entering the room. Discuss readiness tasks such as turning in papers, lunch money procedure, taking attendance, turning in notes from

parents, putting away lunch boxes, hanging up coats, and preparing for class (e.g., sharpening pencils and getting notebooks). In addition, discuss when to sharpen pencils during the school day or where to get pencils and paper if needed.

- **Guided Practice**—Students copy the word webs. This is to be collected and placed in the orientation folder that will be made later in the day. Next, discuss what to do when the rule is broken. For example, forgetting books, pencil, or paper. Discuss solutions. In this way, you introduce high expectations for learning and student accountability.
- **Closure**—Why is being prepared for class important?

The teacher continues to teach the management plan with a discussion of why rules are important to the class. The teacher must reinforce that RULES ALLOW and NOT RESTRICT! (See Figure 4.)

PLANNED LESSONS AND ACTIVITIES

- **Topic**—Our Classroom Rules
- **Opener**—Review the first rule of the class: "Be prepared for class." Suggest that the class discuss why rules are to allow and not restrict or why rules are important.
- **Objectives**—The student will be able to:
  1. list three reasons why rules are important.
  2. develop four more rules that will help me teach and you learn.
- **Instruction**—Ask students what they think would happen if two teams were playing baseball and there were no rules, coach, or umpire. List answers on the board. Discuss rules and why they are important. For younger students, you can discuss ways to make a happy class. On the chalk board, list three to five ways we can have a happy, safe class. For older students, you can tell them that you selected the first rule, "Be prepared for class," and that they are going to choose the four additional rules for this class. Discuss the need for rules to be clearly stated, short in length, positively stated, and easy to memorize.
- **Guided Practice**—For older students, assign students to groups of four and each group will think of four rules that are needed in this classroom. Give a time limit for the work to be completed. Instead of group work, each student can write four more rules he or she would like to have in the classroom. List these rules on the chalk board.

Then let the students select the rules, and agree on the rules. A vote is taken for commitment to the class rules. A poster and/or bulletin board is made of the class rules.

- **Closure**—Why are rules important? Give me three reasons. How can rules help me teach? How can rules help you learn?
- **Independent Practice**—Write the five rules to include in orientation folders.

Figure 4. Classroom Rules

Develop classroom rules:

1. Use approximately five rules.
2. State them clearly.
3. Make them short and easy to memorize.
4. State them positively.
5. Get a commitment to the rules (show of hands, vote, contract, bulletin board display).
6. Teach each rule (share expectations).

Teach classroom rules:

1. Involve the students in the development of the rules.
2. Discuss and internalize their value.
3. Discuss expectations.
4. Get student agreement and commitment to rules (vote, contract).
5. Teach rules.
6. Model rules.
7. Review rules.
8. Reinforce rules.
9. Monitor whether or which rules have been learned.
10. Reteach if necessary.
11. Enforce rules.
12. Correct/Consequences/Conference.

(Figure 4 continued →)

(Figure 4 continued)

Sample rules:

1. Be prepared. 2. Be cooperative. 3. Be respectful. 4. Be responsible.	1. Be prepared to learn. 2. Encourage others. 3. Use quiet voices. 4. Give full attention to the teacher when he or she is speaking.
1. Be prepared for class. 2. Treat each other fairly. 3. Follow teacher requests. 4. Obey all school rules. 5. Work to do your best.	1. Come to class prepared to work and learn. 2. Be considerate of others. 3. Respect others' property. 4. Speak with an inside voice. 5. Obey all school rules.

Set up procedures for:

1. Routines for the beginning of the school day, ending of the school day.
2. Cues for gaining student attention.
3. Turning in assignments (in proper baskets).
4. Handing notes to the teacher (in the special basket on the teacher's desk).
5. Turning in late work.
6. Using notebooks for each subject (taking notes).
7. Appropriate times to sharpen pencils.
8. Using passes—hall, bathroom, office, nurse.
9. Appropriate auditorium and lunchroom behavior.
10. Fire drills.
11. Classroom visitors.
12. Doing make-up work due to illness.
13. Solving problems.

ESTABLISH AFTER-LUNCH ROUTINE: Read-aloud time. Select reading material to read to the class for approximately fifteen minutes. Decide what you want the students to do while you read.

ACTIVITY: Have students begin to make an orientation folder of information pertaining to this class. The folder can contain handouts, notes, a schedule of the day, a calendar, school policies and rules, important dates, and curriculum highlights. The student adds information and assignments to the folder throughout the week. The folders are kept in a special location in the room. At completion of the folder, the student signs a contract that he or she understands his or her role in the teaching and learning process as well as understands the operation of the class and the teacher's management plan that will maximize student learning and minimize disruptive student behavior.

The students take home the folder during the second week of school and familiarize their parents with the class process. Parents sign a statement that the student has briefed them concerning the classroom management plan.

ACTIVITY: Distribute the activity for the orientation folder (Figure 5) to the students. Circulate around the room as they are completing this assignment. Ask students to share their feelings. For younger students this can be done orally or they can draw pictures. Older students can write a descriptive paragraph about how they feel about school and learning. Collect the assignment and read responses; later put the ditto, picture, or paragraph in the orientation folders.

Figure 5. Activity for the Orientation Folder

More About Me

1. What is your favorite holiday and why do you like it?
2. Who is your favorite friend? Why?
3. What do you like most about your home? Why?
4. What is your favorite thing to eat?
5. What do you like to do (or) what is your favorite thing to do?
6. Tell about a special gift you have received from someone.
7. What is something you have never done and would like to try? Why?
8. Tell about a good dream.
9. What is your favorite story and why do you like it?
10. What makes you mad?

PLANNED LESSONS AND ACTIVITIES

Use the established cue to gain everyone's attention.

- **Topic**—Get to Know Your Classmates
- **Opener**—How do you feel when you walk into a room and you do not know anyone? How do you feel when you go somewhere and you see lots of your friends?
- **Objectives**—The student will be able to:
  1. identify three reasons for getting to know his or her classmates.
  2. name and know something about two, four, or six classmates.
- **Instruction**—Begin by asking the students if they know everyone in the class. Ask a specific student to name as many of the students as he or she can. Discuss why it is important to know each other in the class—they are more comfortable, accepted, more like a group, and so on.
- **Closure**—John, Why is it important to know people in this class? Mary, tell me the name of one of the friends we learned about today or the four friends we got to know today? Tell the class something about one or all four. Ask a few students to name these friends and tell something they learned about them. Tell them that they will do this activity each day until everyone knows everyone else by name and knows something about each person.

  Each time this activity is repeated, review the names of the students previously spotlighted by having those students stand up at the beginning of the activity and quizzing the class to see if they can remember their names and something about them. (For other ideas for get-acquainted activities, see Figure 6. For two actual activities, see Figures 7 and 8.)

ACTIVITY: Set aside some time to take the students on a tour of the school. Help students become familiar with the different areas in the school: office, library, and gymnasium. In addition, show them the offices of the counselor, nurse, custodian, secretary, and principal. Help students learn their names. The final stop is the cafeteria as you take them to lunch.

Figure 6. Ideas for Get-Acquainted Activities

1. Class names BINGO.

2. Show-and-Tell Suitcase—Student gives name and where he or she is going and one thing he or she is going to take along. Each student repeats what has been said before and adds his or her name and an item.

3. Name Chain. Students sit in a circle and share their names and something about themselves or a way that others can remember them or their names. A ball of string or a bean bag can be used to toss to the next student to share. Suggest that students remember who they toss the string to for making a bulletin board display of this activity.

4. Interview classmates.

5. Scavenger Hunt to find out things about classmates: Who has a cat? Who has a birthday in April?

6. Find a Friend. Write down three things about yourself and find classmates that have the same things in common with you.

7. Prepared dittos that have things written on them to find out about classmates.

8. Collect signatures of students who agree with certain written statements such as "I like baseball," "I try to do my very best," and "I always turn on the radio when I study." Students and/or teachers can create these statements.

Figure 7. Get-Acquainted Activity

Let's Get Acquainted

Try to use the names of all your classmates to fill in the boxes. For example, look at the first box. It says: Has black hair. Find a student with black hair. Write his or her name in that box.

1. Has black hair	2. Middle name is the same as yours	3. Favorite color is blue
4. Loves to write	5. Likes vegetables	6. Shoe size is the same as yours
7. Has a cat	8. Is taller than you are	9. Is wearing tennis shoes
10. Plays a sport	11. Went to the zoo this summer	12. Wants to be famous
13. Has a garden	14. Likes to draw	15. Has an older brother

Figure 8. Get-Acquainted Activity

Interview Me

In pairs, take turns asking each other the following questions. Write the responses on a piece of paper. Circle the similar responses. Chart your similarities and differences. Class data can be graphed and placed on a bulletin board.

1. What are your favorite school subjects?

2. What is your favorite sport to play?

3. What makes you happy?

4. How many pets do you have?

5. What is your favorite movie? Why?

6. What kinds of food do you like to eat?

7. What is something you have never done before?

8. What countries have you visited?

9. What do you like most about your school? Why?

10. What do you like to do after school?

ESTABLISH A ROUTINE FOR THE END OF THE DAY: Closure is a must to end every day. Set aside ten to fifteen minutes each day: for younger students, possibly once just before lunch and again before the end of the day; for older students, once at the end of the day.

Simple closure activities include the following: "Tell me one thing you learned today." "Tell me what you enjoyed most today?" "Tell me something you learned today that you want to tell your mom, dad, brother, sister, or friend." "Tell me something you learned today that your brother or sister doesn't know. "Tell me something interesting about science." "Tell me something you are thinking about when I say... (pick a topic taught during the day)." Then ask them to complete these sentences about today's learning: "Today I learned..., I relearned..., and I wish..."

GUIDELINES: Pass out an introductory letter (Figure 9) to go home to the parents and attach it to the prepared list of materials and supplies needed for class.

Figure 9. Introductory letter

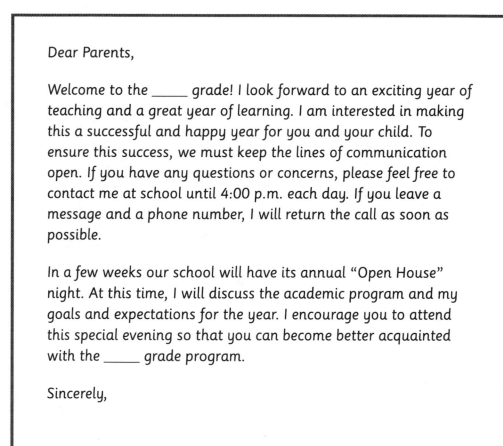

Dear Parents,

Welcome to the _____ grade! I look forward to an exciting year of teaching and a great year of learning. I am interested in making this a successful and happy year for you and your child. To ensure this success, we must keep the lines of communication open. If you have any questions or concerns, please feel free to contact me at school until 4:00 p.m. each day. If you leave a message and a phone number, I will return the call as soon as possible.

In a few weeks our school will have its annual "Open House" night. At this time, I will discuss the academic program and my goals and expectations for the year. I encourage you to attend this special evening so that you can become better acquainted with the _____ grade program.

Sincerely,

REMINDERS:
- ✔ Identify several classroom routines.
- ✔ Label trays or baskets to collect students' work. Use labels such as Teacher, In, Homework, as well as labels for subjects, such as Math or English. The Teacher basket is for notes from parents, attendance sheets, and homework recording forms.
- ✔ Prepare a poster of rules.
- ✔ Read "More About Me" worksheet.
- ✔ Prepare a map of the school.
- ✔ Get a journal that someone has written to read to the class.

DAY 2—SET HIGH EXPECTATIONS

BEGIN THE DAY: Greet the students at the door.

OPENING ACTIVITIES: Place reminders on the board for the students to follow.
1. Get your name tags.
2. Get prepared for class.
3. Sit in your seat.
4. Be ready to say the Pledge of Allegiance and have a silent moment.

ESTABLISH A ROUTINE PROCEDURE AND ACTIVITY TO BEGIN EACH DAY:
Establish what the students need to do each day when they come into the classroom. This procedure remains the same throughout the year. The routine procedure for every morning is for the students to first get prepared for class upon entering the room and then have a routine activity.

Many teachers start each day with tasks the student must do in order to be prepared to begin the school day. Then, they establish a routine activity such as quotes to read, discuss, and evaluate; comics to be shared; journals to be kept; or a silent sustained reading (SSR) activity for ten minutes. (Other routine activities and procedures are listed in Figure 10.)

You need to establish and teach at least three routine procedures and activities: one to begin the day, one after lunch, and one to end the day. The routine activity for beginning the day in this management plan is journal writing for ten minutes. For younger students, you may want them to do a picture web, in which you introduce a word and the students draw pictures of what the word means to them.

Begin today by teaching the routine procedure and activity. Lead the students through the routine procedure of getting prepared for class and writing in

Figure 10. Routine Activities and Procedures

Routine activities are designed for success and to insure that everyone participates. Routine activities that can help you structure your day are:

1. Write in a journal.
2. Write the quote for the day and what the quote means to you.
3. Write the learning objective for the day in a notebook.
4. Write in a vocabulary notebook the vocabulary words for the day.
5. Use sustained silent reading time.

After-lunch routine procedures include the following:

1. Read-aloud time (story).
2. Silent sustained reading.
3. Report and discuss current events.
4. Social issue discussion.
5. Free time/catch-up time.
6. Student focus.
7. Independent time (to use the computer, go to a learning center, go to the library, or read).
8. Committee work for class project.

Possible end-of-the-day routine procedures:

1. Closure activity.
2. Review activities, trivia strategy, (or) games.
3. Write homework assignments in notebooks.
4. Free time/catch-up time.
5. Write in a learning log.

their journal. The content of the lesson might be learning the value of journal writing. You could begin to teach them about several people who have kept journals and how that has influenced history, science, and other people as well as their own lives. An activity can be to make a cover for their journals and record entry dates for the first month. The routine procedure is used to begin the day, begin the block of time, or begin the subject matter course.

USE CUE: Use a cue, for example, a raised hand and move to the front of the room. Get everyone's attention before beginning to teach the lesson and/or give out information. Use strong and direct eye contact for compliance.

GUIDELINES: Teach the students the fire drill firsts: lights out, windows closed, door closed, the line-up procedure (by rows), and the route out of building and to the designated area outside of building. Have a mock fire drill to practice procedures. For the line-up procedure, tell each student to remember the child who belongs in front of him or her and in back of him or her so that when you get outside to the designated area, the students can tell you if someone is missing or students can find their buddies once they get to the designated area.

PLANNED LESSONS AND ACTIVITIES

Use the established cue to gain everyone's attention. Teach one or two classroom rules a day until all rules have been taught. Rules should be taught just as if they were curriculum topics. Plan the lesson to include Topic, Opener, Objectives, Instruction, Discussion, Activities, Check for Understanding, Guided Practice, Closure, and Independent Practice. The next lesson to teach includes the second rule of showing respect for one another.

- **Topic**—Rule 2: Show Respect to One Another
- **Opener**—Brainstorm for ideas about the word *respect.* Explore such ideas as being polite, helping others, treating others fairly, not touching others' property, and the golden rule.
- **Objectives**—The student will be able to:
  1. define the word respect.
  2. demonstrate respect in situations.
  3. provide examples of respect.
- **Instruction**—The students read the definition of respect. The teacher puts two columns on the board: What is respect and What is not respect. The teacher presents situations such as showing respect at home, showing respect in school, showing respect on the playground, and showing respect while playing baseball. The students begin to understand what respect means, what it looks like, and what it feels like.
- **Check for Understanding**—Present a situation and ask if this is a situation where respect is shown. Ask students to show a thumbs up or stand up or raise their hand. Scan the class and if the majority understand, move to the second objective.
- **Guided Practice**—The younger students can give examples of respect. Older students can work in pairs and write two examples of respect on an index card. Then they can share or role play a few examples. Collect the cards to use for reviewing the rule.

- **Closure**—How can you show respect to the teacher? How can you show respect to your classmates? How can respect be a part of our class?
- **Independent Practice**—For older students—give them an assignment to look for two examples of respect and disrespect (at home, in sports, and so on). Tell them that the class will discuss them tomorrow.

ACTIVITY: Give out textbooks, if available, the first or second day. Then introduce the students to the new textbooks. Along with the textbooks, give out an index card. Have students write their name on the top of the card and then list each book received and its inventory number. Collect the cards .

Have students fill out another index card and place their name, address, phone number, birthday, and the last name of the person or persons they are living with at this address. This card is for your reference and for you to take home and be able to make calls to students and/or students' families.

AFTER-LUNCH ROUTINE: Read aloud to the students. To follow up on the routine procedure of journal writing, begin reading journals written by famous people.

PLANNED LESSONS AND ACTIVITIES

Use the established cue to gain everyone's attention. The teacher begins to discuss and teach the need for consequences to support the classroom rules.
- **Topic**—Correction Plan
- **Opener**—Review the class rules and give examples of inappropriate behaviors and have the students name the rule that is being broken.
- **Objectives**—The student will be able to:
  1. list three reasons why correction is needed.
  2. describe the hierarchy of correction.
  3. create situations where correction is needed.
  4. plan a role play using the correction plan.
- **Instruction**—Discuss the need for a correction plan. Discuss the need for a hierarchy of consequences. Teach your correction plan. Go through the four steps (listed below) and demonstrate what it looks like to be remindd that a rule is not being followed. Inform the students that if something happens such as fighting, the teacher immediately jumps to Step 4 and the student is removed from the

classroom. Select a student to get help if such a situation develops in the classroom.

Below each step are suggested ways of carrying out the step. The teacher decides which suggestions to use and how many to offer in each category. The third and fourth steps must be consequences that the students don't like or they will take you to that level too often (see Figure 11 for a list of consequences). The correction plan is outlined below:

A. Step 1—Nonverbal cues
1. eye contact.
2. proximity.
3. body language.
4. hand signal.

B. Step 2—Verbal cues
1. Use the student's name.
2. Use an "I" statement (Billy, I need your attention now because I only have ten more minutes of class).
3. Use words such as "Stop," "Check Yourself," or a word or phrase the students select to signal inappropriate behavior that must be stopped.

C. Step 3—Time out
1. Student goes to the assigned place in the room.
2. Student goes to an assigned place in the room and writes in the behavior notebook what rule he or she was not following and how to demonstrate more appropriate behavior in the future.
3. Student goes to the designated place out of the room, such as another classroom.

You can use colored index cards to work with the time-out procedure. For example, you will present a colored index card to the student. The color will convey the message and the procedure to follow. A green card means go to the designated time out spot in the room for ten minutes and write in the behavior notebook—name, date, rule student broke, what student learned, and what student will do next time—and then the student will return to his or her seat; a yellow card means go to the designated time-out spot in the room and write in the behavior notebook and then leave the classroom to work in another teacher's room (prearranged) for ten to fifteen minutes; and a pink card means a conduct notice and the student must go to the teacher's desk, sit in the teacher's chair, write in the behavior notebook, write a letter home to parents explaining the conduct notice, and wait for the teacher to discuss the behavior with him or her before rejoining the class and returning to his or her seat.

D. Step 4—Consequences
1. in-class loss of free time, class detention, after-school time.
2. a conduct notice.
3. call to parent.
4. conference with student, conference with student and parent.
5. send to the principal.
6. school detention, in-school suspension, suspension.

- **Guided Practice**—Break the class into groups and let the students create situations where a correction plan would be needed. The students must plan role plays of the situations and the steps being followed for correction. Post the correction plan on the front wall. Practice with colored cards.
- **Closure**—Why does a teacher need a correction plan? Why does a student need a correction plan? Do we all understand the correction plan and the steps I will be using? Indicate with a thumbs up. (Teacher scans the room to see that all respond.)

PLANNED LESSONS AND ACTIVITIES

Use the established cue to gain everyone's attention. This planned lesson continues as outlined in Day 1 until everyone has been in the spotlight.
- **Topic**—Continue with Get to Know Your Classmates.
- **Opener**—Begin by reviewing the names of students previously spotlighted by having those students stand up at the beginning of the activity and quizzing the class to see if they can remember their names and something about them.
- **Objectives**—The student will be able to:
    1. review names and remember something about the previous students spotlighted.
    2. name and learn something about two/four/six new classmates.
- **Instruction**—Ask the students if they know everyone in the class. Ask a student to name as many of the students that he or she can. Discuss why it is important to know each other in the class. Then ask

the students to take out a piece of paper and fold it in half, twice, or three times to make two, four, or six squares. Explain that for this activity they will have about twenty minutes to choose two, four, or six students to get to know. They are to write in each square of the paper a student's first name and one or two things about him or her. Students must try to tell different things about themselves each time they are asked a question. Tell them you will blow a whistle when it is time to switch and then everyone must find someone else and begin again.

After the students have filled the squares, randomly or selectively choose two or four students to get to know and call out one name at a time. The students who have information on these students share it with the group.

- **Closure**—Ask students why it's important to know people in the class. Ask them to name one of the friends they learned about and something about him or her.

Each time this activity is repeated, review the names of the students previously spotlighted by having those students stand up at the beginning of the activity and quizzing the class to see if they can remember their names and something about them.

Figure 11. List of Consequences

1. Add time after school—alternate this duty with another teacher.
2. Take away free time—alternate with another teacher: one teacher takes students displaying appropriate behavior outside or to her room for fun or free time and the other teacher keeps the students displaying inappropriate behavior to finish an assignment or a consequence assignment.
3. Call for a conference—teacher/student or teacher, student, and parent.
4. Restrict Freedom Fridays.
5. Develop contracts for improving behavior.
6. Use checks, points, or demerits.
7. Give detention.
8. Issue conduct notices.
9. Send to Principal.
10. Send to the counselor.
11. Call parents.

END-OF-THE-DAY ROUTINE: Say to the students: "Tell me one thing you learned about how this class operates?"

GUIDELINES: Plan a "Show and Tell" type of activity. The younger students can bring in something you designate (something small and the next week something red, etc.) to place in a box. Older students can bring in trivia (they can write quotes, riddles, or brain teasers on strips of paper or cut out cartoons from newspapers or magazines and fold and place them in the "Funny Box.") Each day a different student can select something out of the "Funny Box" and share it with the class. Another box called "What's Up?" might be used for news clippings on current events to be collected and read or discussed.

REMINDERS:
- ✔ Get index cards (green, yellow, and pink).
- ✔ Assess students' learning needs.
- ✔ Prepare class schedules.

DAY 3—BE ENTHUSIASTIC

BEGIN THE DAY: Greet students at the door.

OPENING ACTIVITIES: Place reminders on the board for the students to follow.
1. Get your name tags.
2. Get prepared for class.
3. Sit in your seat.
4. Be prepared for the Pledge of Allegiance and a silent moment.

ROUTINE PROCEDURE AND ACTIVITY TO BEGIN EACH DAY: The routine procedure every morning is for the students to first get prepared for class upon entering the room and then to write in their journals for ten minutes. Monitor the routine procedure and give feedback.

USE CUE: Raise your hand and move to the front of the room. Get everyone's attention before beginning the lesson. Use strong and direct eye contact for compliance. Add names to the compliance expectation by saying, "John, I need your attention now." "Mary, do you see the cue? Please, stop talking now." Time the students to see how long it takes to get everyone's attention.

GUIDELINES: Discuss the teacher's goal for how to begin. Describe progress with the morning routine procedure and activity. Give students information such as

"Fifteen students were following the procedures when I scanned the room. That means 50% of you are really catching on to the process. Let's get 100% tomorrow." Develop a class expectation and goal for how to begin class. Discuss the need for other procedures. Begin to think in terms of developing class norms that are appropriate.

Discuss the use of the cue and tell the students how long it takes to get everyone's attention. Tell students what is reasonable and that additional time spent on getting everyone's attention will be taken off of students' time. "If you abuse it, you lose it" or "If you can't handle it, you can't have it." Time taken is time that must be returned. Make students aware that you will be timing them for compliance. If acceptable, the class will receive a reward, if unacceptable, time will be taken from students.

OPENING ACTIVITIES: Explain to the class the method of taking attendance. The students will check themselves in each morning as they walk into the room. Students will insert their name cards into a library pocket, which is on a poster in the back of the room. The name cards are placed on the back table. The students will run through this procedure. Select an attendance helper and go through the procedure. The attendance helper picks up the cards left on the table, fills out the attendance form, and places the form in the "Teacher" Basket. At the end of the day, the student takes all name cards out of pockets and places all cards on the back table for the next day. A similar procedure to take lunch count can be done at the same time.

ACTIVITY: Give each student a map of the school with special areas filled in by you or to be filled in by them. This activity is especially important to younger students and students coming to a new school. Students like to record last year's teacher and mark the room as well as this year's teacher and their new room. An arrow line showing the fire drill route will be on the map. Students will discuss the route, mark the route, and trace the route. One map will be posted in the room and the students will place their map in the orientation folder. Make additional copies to give to new students as they join the class throughout the year to help them feel more secure in a new place.

PLANNED LESSONS AND ACTIVITIES

Use the established cue to gain everyone's attention. Teach one or two classroom rules a day until all rules have been taught.
- **Opener**—Use yesterday's assignment (the students were to look for two examples of respect) to discuss briefly this rule. Then introduce

the next rule.

     Remember, rules should be taught from prepared lesson plans that include the Topic, Opener, Objectives, Instruction, Discussion, Activities, Check for Understanding, Guided Practice, Closure, and Independent Practice.

GUIDELINES: Begin using the textbooks. Most of the information for the first week or two is usually review material. Establish what the students should do when they are finished with their work.

AFTER-LUNCH ROUTINE: Continue to read journal entries written by many different people for different purposes (for example, Anne Frank's journal, war accounts, last days of people).

PLANNED LESSONS AND ACTIVITIES

Use the established cue to gain everyone's attention. Continue to teach correction plan and further explain and demonstrate it. Decide on the procedure for time out.

- **Topic**—Continue with Correction Plan.
- **Opener**—Review rules by providing examples of a rule not being followed. The student will have to name the rule being broken and give the steps to the correction plan.
- **Objectives**—The student will be able to:
  1. apply the steps of the correction plan when class rules are not followed.
  2. describe Step 3 (time out) of the correction plan.
  3. fill in the required information on a behavior notebook page.
- **Instruction**—Discuss Step 3 of the correction plan. What is time out? Can you think when a time out is used in sports? What is a time-out chair? What does it mean to go to your room? Why is a time-out period important? Have you ever needed a time out? The time out used in this class is important. If anyone gets to Step 3 you must write in the behavior notebook. It will be placed at the designated "time out" location. Identify the time-out location and show students the behavior notebook. Ask for a summary of what happens if student is sent to time out.

      Discuss with students the contents of the behavior notebook page. The page includes the following:

Name and date.
What rule did you break?
What did you learn?
What will you do next time?

If a student is referred to the principals office, the behavior notebook may go with him or her for the principal to see. The behavior notebook may be shared with parents. The notebook also serves to document behavior and frequency of such problems.

- **Guided Practice**—Provide an example of a student breaking a rule and demonstrate the steps up to the time-out step. Then give everyone a page from the behavior notebook and have students fill out the page for this student and sign their name. Discuss the process and find out if they had difficulties filling out the page. Let the students share a few pages. Collect these papers.

- **Closure**—What does time out mean? What step of the correction plan is time out? In time out, what questions are you to answer in the behavior notebook? Do you have to get to Step 3? What can you do to stay away from time out? What is Step 1? What is Step 2? What is Step 4?

Use colored index cards to demonstrate the third step (time out procedure). For example, present a colored index card to a student. The color indicates a message and procedure to be followed. In the third step, a green card means go to designated time-out spot in the room for ten minutes and write in behavior notebook—name, date, rule student broke, what student learned, and what student will do next time—and then the student will return to his or her seat; a yellow card means go to the designated time-out spot in the room and write in the behavior notebook and then leave the classroom to work in another teacher's room (prearranged) for ten to fifteen minutes.

A pink card means a conduct notice and the student must go to the teacher's desk, sit in the teacher's chair, write in the behavior notebook, write a letter home to parents explaining the conduct notice, and wait for the teacher to discuss the behavior with him or her before rejoining the class and returning to his or her seat.

PLANNED LESSONS AND ACTIVITIES

Use the established cue to gain everyone's attention. This planned lesson continues as outlined in Day 1 until everyone has been in the spotlight.

- **Topic**—Continue with Get to Know Your Classmates.
- **Opener**—Review the names of the students previously spotlighted by having those students stand up at the beginning of the activity and quizzing the class to see if they can remember their names and something about them.
- **Objectives**—The student will be able to:
  1. recall names and remember something about the students previously spotlighted.
  2. name and learn something about two, four, or six new classmates.

ACTIVITY: Have students write something about themselves on an index card and personalize it by making it look awesome. And have them write their name on the back of the index card. Share the personalized name cards with the class and put the cards on a bulletin board headlined "Who am I? Who are we?" You must write a card too.

END-OF-THE-DAY ROUTINE: Say to students: "Tell me something that you learned as a _____ grader that you didn't know when you were in _____ grade."

GUIDELINES: Remind students to bring certain objects or cartoons, riddles, and quotes to school and put in the "Funny Box."

REMINDERS:
- ✔ Bring a stop watch or timer.
- ✔ Bring colored index cards.
- ✔ Prepare bulletin board.
- ✔ Cut out 50 hands (in white or colored paper) or have students trace hands and cut them out.

DAY 4—BE POSITIVE

BEGIN THE DAY: Greet the students at the door.

OPENING ACTIVITIES: Put a reminder cloud on the board for students to get name tags, take attendance, and be prepared for class. The class will say the Pledge of Allegiance and have a silent moment.

THE FIRST-YEAR TEACHER

ROUTINE PROCEDURE: The routine procedure every morning is for the students to first get prepared for class upon entering the room and next to write in their journals for ten minutes. The teacher monitors students and makes positive comments to the students following the procedure. The teacher says. "I like the way you (name) came into class, finished all the readiness tasks and started writing in your journal."

USE CUE: Raise your hand and move to the front of the room. Continue to use the cue and time the response. Report the time it took for attention to be focused on the teacher. If satisfactory, reward class. If unsatisfactory, take that amount of time from free time, lunch time, fun time, or whatever. Establish an expectation that time wasted is time given to the teacher. "If you abuse it, you lose it." Provide a specific on how this will be done. The students may not need a reward or consequence; they may just enjoy beating the clock or working with the time. Discuss with the class how they can assist each other in following the beginning of class procedures.

ACTIVITY: Place class schedule of times for subjects, specials (Art, Music, Physical Education, Library), and lunch on the chalkboard and discuss it with students. Older students can copy schedule and younger students receive a prepared schedule to include in the orientation folder. A class schedule will also be posted on the side wall.

GUIDELINES: Brainstorm and list jobs needed to make a class run smoothly. Review how attendance is taken. Discuss jobs such as line leader, lunch ticket collector, board washer, office messenger, cafeteria table washers, sweepers, and visitor monitor. Discuss the job descriptions. Assign the jobs to students and have them write their responsibilities on a sheet of paper. Review, discuss, and possibly revise the roles and responsibilities, and have the students write them in their notebooks. Students are accepting and initiating "ownership" in the management of their class.

Also choose a student for the job of "Peer Assistant," a student who will assist students with questions when the teacher is busy. Another job is the "New-Kid-on-the-Block Helper," who helps new students become familiar with class. The "Homework Helper" is a student who records who has turned in the homework. The class may need more assigned jobs as the weeks progress.

Make a bulletin board or poster entitled "Helping Hands" to post jobs as needed and assign students to the jobs. Names for jobs may change as often as you like. The job and the student's name are each placed on hands and put together on the bulletin board.

PLANNED LESSONS AND ACTIVITIES

Use the established cue to gain everyone's attention. The teacher begins to teach the Personal Problem/Solution Plan

- **Topic**—Personal Problem/Solution Plan (PPSP)
- **Opener**—Discuss with the class what kinds of behaviors of other students keep them from learning, concentrating, or feeling good about themselves.
- **Objectives**—The student will be able to:
  1. identify behaviors that interfere with learning.
  2. list three reasons why he or she needs to handle problems.
  3. describe the personal problem/solution plan.
  4. demonstrate situations where the personal problem/solution plan would be needed.
- **Instruction**—Discuss reasons why students need to handle problems or have a method to use in solving problems. Discuss times and instances when all of us might be bothered by the actions of another person (at the movies, in the cafeteria, on the playground). Teach the steps to the personal problem/solution plan (Bosch & Kersey 1993):
  1. First, try ignoring the person who is bothering you. (Put imaginary ear muffs over your ears.) If necessary, turn, look, or if possible, move away from the person.
  2. If that doesn't work, ask the person politely to stop. "I cannot do my work when you are _____."
  3. If that doesn't work, tell the person in a loud voice to "Stop it." "Cut it out." or "I don't like that."
  4. If that doesn't work, ask the teacher if you can talk with him or her in private. (Student could be provided with a yellow card for this step). Arrange a time to talk. Tell the teacher the problem and let him or her offer suggestions.
  5. If that doesn't work, ask the teacher if you can talk to the principal. Talk over the problem with him or her and ask for help in solving the problem permanently. (p. 229) (Reprinted with permission of the Helen Dwight Reid Educational Foundation. Published by Heldref Publications, 1319 18th Street, N.W. Washington D.C. 20036-1802. Copyright 1993.)
- **Guided Practice**—Assign the students to groups and let them name situations in which the personal problem/solution plan would be needed. Then have the students role play the situations and the steps to the plan. Post the Personal Problem/Solution Plan.

- **Closure**—Why do students need to have a personal problem/solution plan? Does everyone understand the steps to take when another person is interfering with your freedom to learn? Show a thumbs up or pat yourself on the back.

AFTER-LUNCH ROUTINE: Teacher reads aloud journals or books that are relevant to current topics of study.

PLANNED LESSONS AND ACTIVITIES

Use the established cue to gain everyone's attention. This planned lesson continues as outlined in Day 1 until everyone has been in the spotlight.
- **Topic**—Continue with Get to Know Your Classmates.
- **Opener**—Review the names of the students previously spotlighted by having those students stand up at the beginning of the activity and quizzing the class to see if they can remember their names and something about them.
- **Objectives**—The student will be able to:
  1. recall names and remember something about the students spotlighted.
  2. name and learn something about two, four, or six new classmates.

END-OF-THE-DAY ROUTINE: Ask students: "How will rules help you in this classroom? Why are rules to allow and not to restrict?"

Review the index cards of examples of respect that the students wrote in a previous lesson.

GUIDELINES: Select a student greeter for a week to join you at the door in the mornings. Post the student greeter's name on the front board. Remind students to bring certain objects or cartoons, riddles, and quotes to school and put them in the "Funny Box" or news clippings of current events for the "What's Up" box.

REMINDERS:
  ✔ Prepare card box (birthday cards, special occasions).

SECOND WEEK

GOAL: REVIEW, MONITOR, AND RETEACH WHAT IS IMPORTANT

Key Teaching Areas:
- ❑ Review Management Plan.
- ❑ Review Rules and Procedures.
- ❑ Review Correction Plan and PPSP.
- ❑ Develop and Teach Incentives.
- ❑ Increase Student Accountability.

Strategies for success:
- ❑ Get the Parent Involved.
- ❑ Provide Get Acquainted Activities.
- ❑ Use Positive Ripple Effect.
- ❑ Use Catch Them Being Good.
- ❑ Provide Praise, Rewards, Feedback, and Encouragement.

REMINDERS:
- ✔ Plain index cards.
- ✔ Buddy card box.

DAY 1—SMILE

BEGIN THE DAY: Teacher and student greeter meet the students in the morning.

OPENING ACTIVITIES: Place the reminder cloud on the board to remind students to get name tags, take attendance, and be prepared for class. Have the class recite the Pledge of Allegiance and have a silent moment. Have students remove the name cards from the bulletin board and collect them. (The cards will be used in Day 2 of the second week.)

ROUTINE PROCEDURE: The routine procedure every morning is for the students to first get prepared for class upon entering the room and then to write in their journals for ten minutes. Monitor this procedure and correct behavior that is inappropriate.

USE CUE: Raise your hand and move to the front of the room. Time how long it takes for everyone's attention. Report or record the time and comment on the amount of student assistance offered to each other. Suggest that "Buddies" help each other. Be consistent in following the process: if satisfactory, reward class; if unsatisfactory, take time away.

ACTIVITY: Assign a buddy to each student. Buddies will change for the second semester. Explain to the students why this is important. Use a "Think, Pair, Share" for the following activity. Let the student buddies get into pairs for approximately five to ten minutes and develop a procedure for being a school buddy. They will write down this information along with address, telephone number, and birthday. Use the "Think Aloud" strategy and let the students share their procedures for all to hear. How many are the same? How many are different? Do you need to change your procedure or add something to your procedure? The responsibilities that need to be discussed thoroughly are what to do if a buddy is absent, has an extended illness, or is celebrating a birthday. For example, the buddy is responsible for getting a card from the card box to send to his or her buddy when it is his or her birthday or to send his or her buddy a card if he or she has an extended illness. Buddies can plan special events and share special news about their buddies.

Think, Pair, Share activities are a great way to begin developing cooperative learning. Start with small groups (pairs) and begin developing the skills needed to work in larger groups and for different purposes. The Think, Pair, Share strategy is quick, usually successful, and can be used anytime. It is especially valuable when a teacher experiences a lack of student participation, energy, or interest. For example, ask pairs to summarize the content so far, fomulate some questions about the material, list advantages of a concept or tell why certain information is important to learn. The teacher must be able to move from whole group instruction to small group instruction as often as needed to keep students engaged in the learning process and focused on the content.

A nonverbal cue or code for forming different group arrangements from pairs to groups of three and four is essential. A hand code may be taught that would signal the students to get into different group arrangements. Holding up two fingers could indicate a Think, Pair, Share activity, three fingers a group of three, four fingers a group of four, index finger a special grouping in which the students are assigned to the group based on ability, and the thumb could be a special group based on student choices of whom they would like to work with. All five fingers raised as well as the hand may indicate stop and all eyes focused on the teacher for further instructions. Remember the signals must be taught and the groups must practice forming quickly as assigned upon each cue before cooperative learning assignments can be made.

GUIDELINES: Review bulletin board or poster of class jobs. Quiz students on jobs and tasks. Also review the Classroom Management Plan (Review Rules and Procedures, Correction Plan, and PPSP).

PLANNED LESSONS AND ACTIVITIES

Use the established cue to gain everyone's attention. The teacher begins to develop and teach incentives to support the classroom rules.

- **Topic**—Incentive Plan
- **Opener**—Ask students what incentives and rewards mean to them. What is your favorite reward? When is a reward given to you? Why is it given?
- **Objectives**—The student will be able to:
  1. dentify rewards for appropriate behavior.
  2. examine situations when rewards are given.
  3. choose three to five rewards to be used in this class.
- **Instruction**—Discuss with students possible incentives for appropriate behavior and academic achievement. Brainstorm ideas for individual and group rewards that a teacher can use in a classroom. Write their ideas on the board under two categories: Individual Rewards and Class Rewards. Discuss the ideas and the situations in which they could be applied. Have the students choose three to five incentives for the class. Keep a list so that different rewards may be earned from time to time or as effectiveness diminishes.
- **Guided Practice**—Present situations and have students decide whether a reward is given. Discuss and explain your expectations.
- **Closure**—Why are rewards important?
- **Independent Practice**—Write the rewards on the board. Have older students copy them and place the copy in their orientation folder. Pass out a reward. Have younger students draw a picture of the reward they like the best. Pass out stickers to each student. (See Figure 12 for list of incentives.)

AFTER-LUNCH ROUTINE: Read aloud to students.

PLANNED LESSONS AND ACTIVITIES

Use the established cue to gain everyone's attention. This planned lesson con

Figure 12. List of Incentives

1. Homework passes.
2. Reward bag.
3. Recognition reinforcers.
4. Ice cream, candies.
5. Freedom Fridays.
6. Parties.
7. Free time.
8. Center time.
9. Activity reinforcers.
10. Token economies.
11. Auctions.
12. Points for pleasure.
13. Lottery.
14. Drawing.
15. "Catch Them Being Good" notes.
16. Marble jar.
17. Secret Word.

tinues as outlined in Day 1 until everyone has been in the spotlight.
- **Topic**—Continue with Get to Know Your Classmates.
- **Opener**—Review the names of the students previously spotlighted by having those students stand up at the beginning of the activity and quizzing the class to see if they can remember their names and something about them.
- **Objectives**—The student will be able to:
  1. recall names and something about the students spotlighted.
  2. name and learn something about two, four, or six new classmates.

END-OF-THE-DAY ROUTINE: Review the rules. Students need to memorize rules and understand that rules have a purpose in their classroom. The students will complete the following sentences.

1. The rule that makes the most sense to me is_____
2. The rule I might change is _____
3. Rules help me by _____

Collect this assignment and place it in the orientation folder. For younger students, take one sentence, discuss it, write it the way they want to complete it, and read it together or copy it.

GUIDELINES: Inform the students that you are going to start calling parents to introduce yourself to them starting this evening and each night this week until all are called. Have them tell their mom, dad, or guardian that you will be calling this week to say hello.

REMINDERS:
- ✔ Begin calling about five parents or guardians each night to say hello and give the date of the "Open House" and to ask for their support for a great year. Let them know you are available and need their input in order to truly be effective. Record the dates of the calls and other information on student index cards.
- ✔ Get colored index cards.
- ✔ Make class roster forms for student helpers to record homework and other tasks.
- ✔ Prepare an assignment sheet.
- ✔ Prepare a calendar.
- ✔ Collect name cards.
- ✔ Prepare "Get Off" forms.

DAY 2—BE REALISTIC: YOU CAN'T DIVIDE YOURSELF INTO 26 PIECES

BEGIN THE DAY: Teacher and student greeter meet the students in the morning.

OPENING ACTIVITIES: Put a reminder cloud on the board to remind students to take attendance, be prepared for class, and to begin the routine procedure. The class will recite the Pledge of Allegiance and have a silent moment.

ROUTINE PROCEDURE: The routine procedure every morning is for the students to first get prepared for class upon entering the room and then to write in their journals for ten minutes. Monitor this procedure. Ask successful students to provide information on how they get prepared. Have a student(s) summarize this information in steps. For example, what they do first, second, and last. Ask if everyone understands (thumbs up), scan the room, and move on to the next thing.

USE CUE: Raise your hand and move to the front of the room. Continue to mon-

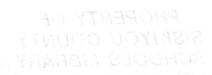

itor amount of time it takes to get everyone's attention.

OPENING ACTIVITIES: Shuffle and pass out the personalized name cards collected previously. A student will stand up and show the back side of the card, which has the name of a student on it. The class will agree or disagree that the name matches the person who was dealt the card. If the students say it's a match and they are correct, the student places the card back on the bulletin board. If it is not a match, the student must find the correct person and the class will again agree or disagree with the match. If a match is made the student puts the card back on the bulletin board. Once this activity is completed, the name cards are to remain on the bulletin board. The class can respond with a "Thumbs Up" if correct and the word "Not" if incorrect.

GUIDELINES: The teacher will prepare an assignment sheet. The assignment sheet is to be used by the students to alert them to what topics or concepts will be taught, the amount of information covered, the requirements and assignments and when they are due. This will enable the student to plan ahead and possibly plan to do the assignments at more convenient times. The teacher explains how the student is held accountable through this assignment sheet and can make appropriate decisions based on his or her needs and time constraints.

Make it clear that assignments that are not completed, will be completed during the school day. Share a philosophy statement, "I accept no excuses, just expect action." Give them an example. If a student comes into the classroom without the homework, what is my expectation? My expectation is that the student must do something about this situation because the assignment was due. I may have to build in time during the school day for unfinished work as well as fun.

Establish a specific day such as the first Monday of the month to pass out assignment sheets and always draw students' attention to information on the sheet. This assignment sheet is important and you have spent considerable time on it so make sure they know the importance of it and your expectations for its use. When you have students focus on the assignment sheet it gives the work a higher priority and sends a message that this is important. The assignment sheet can be prepared weekly or monthly.

For younger students, the teacher will prepare a calendar. This calendar form can be one with all or some information listed. The student can fill in some information as presented. The younger students could fill in a limited amount of information and color or put stickers on key events, dates, birthdays of classmates, and so on. The birthday information should come from the buddy. Remind the buddies of their responsibilities.

An assignment sheet and/or calendar will be included in the orientation folder to alert the parents that this information will be coming home at a certain time (establish a day) to keep them informed. With the students and parents well informed, the teacher can have high expectations for students' learning and parental support.

AFTER-LUNCH ROUTINE: Read aloud to students.

PLANNED LESSONS AND ACTIVITIES

Use the established cue to gain everyone's attention. Begin to teach specific rewards and techniques. You may choose to teach one, two, or possibly all of these techniques.

- **Topic**—"Marble Jar," "Secret Word," "Get Off" Form, and "Catch Them Being Good" Technique. (Omit the "Get Off" form for the younger students.)
- **Opener**—Show the students a jar. Catch someone being good and drop a few marbles in the jar. Next, catch the class doing something good and drop a few more marbles in the jar. Ask students what they think about this marble jar. If you're using "Secret Word," you can introduce this technique by playing the game Hangman.
- **Objectives**—The student will be able to:
  1. explain the use of the "Marble Jar," "Secret Word,"and the "Get Off" form.
  2. recognize the "Catch Them Being Good" technique.
- **Instruction**—Begin by telling the students about the marble jar and its purpose. Give specific examples of how to earn marbles.

  Discuss the "Secret Word." The class decides on a positive reward for using appropriate behavior. When the teacher notes good behavior, the teacher writes the first letter of the reward on the chalkboard. When the word is spelled the students receive the reward. Explain that you will "catch them being good" when rules and procedures are followed, when students respond immediately to your cue, when students are kind, considerate, and helpful to one another, or giving 100% or more to a situation. Remind the students that the rewards they choose must be realistic and practical. Tell the class that once the marble jar is filled or the secret word is spelled, the reward is given, and we start again with an empty marble jar or another word.
- **Guided Practice**—Have students write down possible class rewards on a slip of paper and collect the slips. The teacher will tally the responses and announce the class reward the next day.

- **Instruction**—The teacher explains the "Get Off" form. This form is a reward that is given to a student who is caught being good. The form entitles the student to "get out" of an assignment. For example, the student may use the form to get out of homework or an inclass assignment. The student simply turns it in to the teacher in place of the assignment. The student may save the forms to use at a later date; however, only one form a day is allowed.
- **Guided Practice**—Have the students summarize the procedure on how to use the "Get Off" form.
- **Closure**—What is the purpose of the marble jar? How many think we will be able to fill this jar? What is the "Secret Word" technique? How many of you plan to get a "Get Off" form? Several forms? Explain the "Catch Them Being Good" technique?
- **Independent Practice**—Have students write a paragraph or verbally explain the "Marble Jar," "Secret Word," "Get Off" form, and "Catch Them Being Good" technique. If students write a paragraph, place it in their orientation folders.

END-OF-THE-DAY ROUTINE: Use a concept webbing idea to review the day's learning. Make sure the correction plan is reviewed at this time.

GUIDELINES: Remind the students that you are going to call parents each night until all are called to introduce yourself. Tell them to tell their mom, dad, or guardian that you will be calling this week to say hello. They should expect your call.

REMINDERS:
- ✔ Prepare contract ditto.
- ✔ Remember "Funny Box" or "What's Up" box.
- ✔ Bring cans.
- ✔ Continue to call about five parents or guardians each night to say hello and give the date of the "Open House" and to ask for their support for a great year. Let them know you are available and need their input in order to truly be effective.

DAY 3—BE FLEXIBLE

BEGIN THE DAY: Teacher and student greeter meet the students in the morning.

OPENING ACTIVITIES: Put the reminder cloud on the board to remind students to take attendance, be prepared for class, and to begin the routine procedure. The class will recite the Pledge of Allegiance and have a silent moment.

ROUTINE PROCEDURE: The routine procedure every morning is for the students to first get prepared for class upon entering the room and then to write in their journals for ten minutes. Continue to monitor. If the majority are following the procedure appropriately, then reteaching is not necessary. If a few students are having difficulty with the routine procedure, reteach it to them and give free time to the majority as a reward. You must reinforce what you expect and what you require.

USE CUE: Raise your hand and move to the front of the room.

GUIDELINES: Have students complete their first writing sample to be placed in a "Performance Portfolio" by completing these sentences: I can..., I'm proud of..., Last year, I learned..., This year I want to learn.... More sentences can be added and more complex ones written if working with an advanced class or a higher grade level. An alternative to the sentence completion is to write a paragraph or story from an uncompleted sentence. Have two or three sentences listed and the student can select one to begin the paragraph or story. Each portfolio consists of a large folder for each student that is placed in a key location in the classroom. The portfolios represent the work students do across time. The student can evaluate his or her progress.

Younger students can make a picture of themselves or their family. They could color a picture of the school or draw a picture of their classroom. Another idea for younger students is to have them make an "I Can" can (from Jones & Jones 1990). The teacher will have collected many cans, removed the labels, and will pass them out to the students. The students will be instructed to decorate their can. Each time the student masters something, he or she writes it down on a piece of paper (or the teacher writes it down) and rolls up the paper, ties a string around it, and places it in the can. Once a month, the student takes the can home to share with parents.

AFTER-LUNCH ROUTINE: Read aloud to students.

GUIDELINES: During an activity from the day before, the students were asked to write down possible group rewards that they would like when the marble jar is filled or when the secret word is completed. The teacher announces the reward chosen by the majority.

PLANNED LESSONS AND ACTIVITIES

Use the established cue to gain everyone's attention. Continue with the incentive part of the correction plan by introducing contracts.

- **Topic**—Contracts
- **Opener**—If you were a teacher, what would you do if you saw that one student did not need to do as many math problems as most of the class? What would you do if you saw that some students simply could not do all the work assigned because they work at a slower pace but yet they understand the process? These students would be receiving a grade of F or Incomplete. Does this really tell me what they can do and what they know?
- **Objectives**—The student will be able to:
  1. describe the use of contracts in this classroom.
  2. explain the contract procedure.
- **Instruction**—Lead the students in a discussion of solutions to meeting learning needs. List the solutions on the board. If contracts are not a part of the discussion, you must introduce this concept. Teach them how contracts will be used in the classroom. The contracts are for three distinct purposes: learning differences, enrichment opportunities, and changing behavior. Provide examples of use in the three areas. Ask the students for examples. Explain the contract procedure and that you will be making these decisions based on student needs. Tell the students that this is a teacher decision and is not open to discussion. Remind them that everyone will be under contract at some time during the year, maybe more than once. Much of the recording and monitoring of contracts is done with forms and checklists, which a student helper or parent volunteer can do. The contract is initially drawn up between a student and teacher for a period of time and discussed thoroughly. Put the contract in a file folder for ease in recording information on the inside of the folder.
- **Guided Practice**—Each student can fill out a contract and the necessary forms. The teacher can use transparencies to highlight the form and information. The students sign and date the form and place it in the Performance Portfolios. (A sample contract can be seen in Figure 13.)
- **Closure**—What are contracts? Why are they important? What are the three uses of contracts in this classroom? Give me some information on the contract procedure?

Figure 13. Sample Contract

The Contract

Student's Name _____

Teacher's Name _____

Parent's Name _____

Date _____

Contract Purpose: _____

_____

The teacher promises to: _____

_____

The student promises to: _____

_____

The parent promises to: _____

My goal is to: _____

_____

END-OF-THE-DAY ROUTINE: Ask students what choice has to do with the correction plan. The student can make a choice to change the inappropriate behavior for appropriate behavior before the teacher directs a behavior change through consequences (Steps 3 and 4). You can use the "Think, Pair, Share" activities during closure as well.

GUIDELINES: Remind the students that you are going to call parents each night until all students are called to introduce yourself. Tell them to tell their mom, dad, or guardian that you will be calling this week to say hello.

REMINDERS:

✔ Remember the "Funny Box" or "What's Up" box.

✔ Remember the "Marble Jar."

✔ Remember index cards.

✔ Prepare strips of paper.

✔ Continue to call about five parents or guardians each night to say hello and to give the date of the "Open House" and to ask for their support for a great year.

✔ Prepare contract management plans.

DAY 4—HAVE A SENSE OF HUMOR · · · · · · · · · · · · · · · ·

BEGIN THE DAY: Teacher and student greeter meet the students in the morning.

OPENING ACTIVITIES: Place the reminder cloud on the board to remind students to take attendance, be prepared for class, and to begin the routine procedure. The class will recite the Pledge of Allegiance and have a silent moment.

ROUTINE PROCEDURE: The routine procedure every morning is for the students to first get prepared for class upon entering the room and then write in their journals for ten minutes.

USE CUE: Raise your hand and move to the front of the room. Continue to monitor the amount of time it takes to get everyone's attention. If the students take too much time, take time from the students to reinforce this procedure.

GUIDELINES: The class will have the opportunity to ask questions about the management plan. For younger students, see how much they have memorized. For older students, review the management plan by putting it into outline form or steps. Follow this progression of concepts: rules, teacher's expectations, correction plan steps, teacher's expectations, and incentives. Discuss the role of the student and the role of the teacher to insure a positive learning environment that maximizes learning potential and minimizes disruptions.

You should have prepared a contract of the management plan that includes the class rules, correction plan, consequences, and incentives and rewards. The student should read it carefully before signing the contract. At the bottom of the contract, the student signs the statement "I _____(name) agree to abide by this contract management plan."

The students are to take their orientation folders home and as a homework assignment discuss the folder and contract with their parents and return the contract tomorrow signed by the parents. Offer a reward for "Next Day Delivery" of the signed contracts. After you receive the signed contract, make two additional copies. The copies are for the parents, teacher, and student.

AFTER-LUNCH ROUTINE: Read aloud to students.

PLANNED LESSONS AND ACTIVITIES

Use the established cue to gain everyone's attention. The teacher continues to prepare students to work together and learn together.

- **Topic**—Cooperative Learning
- **Opener**—Discuss the saying, "Two heads are better than one." This class is going to work together and learn together.
- **Objectives**—The student will be able to:
  1. list three advantages of cooperative learning.
  2. project three disadvantages of cooperative learning.
  3. propose solutions to the disadvantages of cooperative learning.
- **Instruction**—Demonstrate cooperative learning by giving one student a list of three words and a dictionary. Pick three more students and give them the same list of three words and three dictionaries. Tell the class that these three will work together and the other student will work alone. They must look up the words and write on a piece of paper the page number found or phonetic spelling and the first definition. Give them a signal to begin. While this is being done, ask the other students, "Who do you think will finish first? Why? Ask the participants how they felt. Have the students focus on the word cooperation. Brainstorm three advantages of cooperative learning. Discuss possible disadvantages and solutions. Place information on the board in three columns: Advantages, Disadvantages, Solutions. Have students take notes. Monitor to make sure they are taking notes. Place these notes in the orientation folder.
- **Closure**—What do you think is the greatest advantage of cooperative learning? What does cooperation mean to you?

END-OF-THE-DAY ROUTINE: Say to students: "Give me a situation where the Personal Problem/Solution Plan (PPSP) might be needed."

A closure game is fun and full of review for tomorrow, last day of the week. The classroom management plan or subject content can be reviewed. Prepare ahead of time strips of paper on which you have written the concepts you have taught. Have students select a strip and tell something about it.

GUIDELINES: Establish a procedure to turn in homework and identify the place to put "Homework" and remind the "Homework" helper to collect and record the homework that is completed on the form. The homework recording form is placed in the "Teacher" basket first thing in the morning. The contract is the first official homework.

Remind the students that you are going to call parents each night until all are called.

REMINDERS:
- ✔ Remember "Funny Box" or "What's Up" box.
- ✔ Remember "Marble Jar."
- ✔ Bring ingredients for a peanut butter sandwich.
- ✔ Continue to call about five parents or guardians each night to say hello and to give the date of the "Open House" and to ask for their support for a great year. Let them know you are available and need their input in order to truly be effective.

DAY 5—TGIF

BEGIN THE DAY: Teacher and student greeter meet the students in the morning.

OPENING ACTIVITIES: Place a reminder cloud on the board or a poster for students to put homework in the "Homework" basket. The student assigned to check homework assignments must record information on the "Homework" form and place it in the "Teacher" basket.

ROUTINE PROCEDURE: The routine procedure every morning is for the students to first get prepared for class upon entering the room and then to write in their journals for ten minutes. Continue to monitor and reward if possible.

USE CUE: Raise your hand and move to the front of the room.

GUIDELINES: Report the number of students turning in the first homework assignment—the contract—on the due day and how many still must turn in their homework assignment. Discuss the homework policy. Share your expectations for the homework assignments. Discuss the importance of homework. Tell them, "My teaching style is not to give a failing grade or an Incomplete but to make sure that the work assigned is understood and completed." Review the homework policy that time will be provided for those students who have not finished their home-work. Those students who have completed their work will be given free time or fun time. The students will review this procedure by performing the following role play described below:

> *Student:* "Mrs. James, I don't have my homework. I left it on the bus."
> *Teacher:* "Okay, what can you do about this?"
> *Student:* "I can do it now before class, at the scheduled time during the day, or if I finish today's work."
> *Teacher:* "Which one are you going to do?"
> *Student:* "I'm going to do it right now."

To support the homework policy, select two days a week to assign homework. Inform the parents of the two days that homework will be assigned. Give interest-ing homework assignments and use creative approaches such as asking students to complete all the odd-numbered problems, the first five, the last five, boys do even, girls do odd; and possibly, add choice by giving two assignments and allowing the students to choose one.

AFTER-LUNCH ROUTINE: Read aloud to students

PLANNED LESSONS AND ACTIVITIES

Use the established cue to gain everyone's attention. Continue to promote cooperative learning. Support the process with a specific procedure to follow:
- **Topic**—Guidelines for Giving Directions
- **Opener**—What are some of your favorite things to eat? How do you make a cake? Who assembled your bike? Everyone needs directions. Sometimes directions are difficult to understand. Directions in this class are made simpler through a procedure. Let's learn the proce-dure.
- **Objectives**—The student will be able to:
  1. examine the importance of understanding directions.
  2. describe the procedure for giving directions.
- **Instruction**—Ask the students "What are some ways directions can be improved?" Write down the students' ideas on the board. Pass out index cards and ask each student to write directions for making a peanut butter and jelly sandwich. Collect the cards. Select a card and have a student read the first direction, pass the card to another stu-

dent to read the second direction, and continue until all directions have been read. Demonstrate making the sandwich by following their directions. The students will begin to see the need for directions to be clear, specific, and given in an ordered way. Introduce the "Guidelines for Giving Directions" that will be used in this classroom. Show the class a transparency or a poster that you have prepared with the list of steps (see below). Describe the steps in detail.

The steps include the following (Bosch 1991):

1. *Provide specific and simply stated directions.*
   a. break down directions into steps.
   b. if there are more than three steps, put directions on a poster, board, handout, or transparency for the students to refer to during the task.

2. *Teach the steps one at a time.*
   a. use discussions, explanations, and examples.
   b. use the "give and get" process—the teacher gives directions and gets the directions back from the students before moving to next step.

3. *Establish a cue that tells the students to stop and shift attention to the teacher.*

4. *Set a time limit for the assignment.*

5. *Inform the students of the evaluation (turned in, graded, exchanged papers or discussed).*
   a. use an individual assignment.
   b. use a group assignment.

6. *Ask if there are any questions. Tell students if they don't understand, they must ask questions now. Questions will not be taken after this time.*

7. *If the students will be working in groups, assign members and pass out work.*

8. *Give students time to begin their work independently before monitoring their work.*

You will have made a poster of the "Guidelines for Giving Directions," which is placed on the board. The students will be able to follow the steps while you are giving directions. You will use the steps each time you give directions for individual assignments and cooperative learning activities. The most important steps are the "give and get" step and the step asking if there are any questions? Remember, when you have gone through the steps and students have started the activity and they have questions, stop the activity and return to the steps emphasizing the step when to ask questions. And say "Now, are we ready to begin?" You must teach, stop, and reteach the procedure to make it work, and to increase and maintain students' accountability to the process.

- **Closure**—Why are directions important? How am I going to give directions to you? How can you make sure you understand the directions?

(Ideas reprinted with permission. Published by National Middle School Association. Copyright 1991.)

END-OF-THE-DAY ROUTINE: Use the closure game you prepared for review. Have students select a strip on which you have written a concept that you have taught. Then they tell something about the concept. Jeopardy, Name that Concept, and Wheel of Fortune are other examples of game formats that you can use.

GUIDELINES: Select a student greeter for a week to join you at the door in the mornings. Post the student greeter's name on the front board.

REMINDERS:
- ✔ Remember "Funny Box" or "What's Up" box.
- ✔ Remember "Marble Jar."
- ✔ Prepare student interest survey.
- ✔ Continue to call about five parents or guardians each night to say hello and to give the date of the "Open House" and to ask for their support for a great year. Let them know you are available and need their input in order to truly be effective.

THIRD WEEK

GOALS: REINFORCE WHAT IS IMPORTANT

Key Teaching Areas:
- ❑ Reinforce Management Plan.
- ❑ Review Correction Plan and PPSP.
- ❑ Review Consequences.
- ❑ Review Incentives.
- ❑ Strengthen Peer Relationships.
- ❑ Develop Group Cohesiveness.
- ❑ Introduce Class Meetings.

Success Strategies:
- ❑ Use Grandma's Rule—First eat your dinner (do your work) and then you can have dessert (reward).
- ❑ Be Fair, Firm, and Friendly.
- ❑ Practice "With-it-ness."
- ❑ Provide Class Rewards.
- ❑ When things are going wrong, stop activities and lessons, go back to Management Plan, and review or reteach Rules and Procedures.

DAY 1—MAKE "GUIDELINES FOR GIVING DIRECTIONS" WORK

BEGIN THE DAY: Teacher and student greeter meet the students in the morning.

OPENING ACTIVITIES: Place the reminder cloud on the board to remind students to take attendance, be prepared for class, and to begin the routine procedure. Inform the students that we no longer need the reminders for how to begin class. Ask the students for the procedure, step by step if necessary.

ROUTINE PROCEDURE: The routine procedure every morning is for the students to first get prepared for class upon entering the room and then to write in their journals for ten minutes.

USE CUE: Raise your hand and move to the front of the room. Continue to monitor amount of time it takes to get everyone's attention. If students take too much time, take time from students to reinforce this procedure.

GUIDELINES: Review "Guidelines for Giving Directions" and use this procedure for all directions that are given to the students. Especially important are the "give and get" step and the step asking if there are any questions? Remember, stop the activity if directions were not understood or questions were asked after the steps were finished and go back to the proper step for the procedure and reteach it. Students usually dislike going over items more than once and catch on quickly.

ACTIVITY: With your students, review your teaching style, which is influenced by student input. Discuss survey data and the use of such information. Review the concept of choice. Prepare students to respond to the interest survey with information that will be useful to the class, the student, and the teacher. Pass out the interest survey. Allow them enough time to complete the survey and have a student from each row collect the surveys. You can use information from the interest survey when greeting students in the mornings. You can also use the survey information to plan interest areas, centers, projects, and select library books or feature books for the classroom. The students' responses can help you plan more interesting, relevant instruction. Your survey data will be used for a later activity.

AFTER-LUNCH ROUTINE: Read aloud to students. Begin to alternate this read-aloud time with Sustained Silent Reading (SSR) or Drop Everything And Read (DEAR) time. Before moving to this SSR or DEAR time, students must have had an opportunity to go to the library or have a well-stocked and relevant inclass library to get books or magazines to read. For younger students, let them get a book(s) or magazine(s) to look at the pictures and predict what the story may be about.

ACTIVITY: Have the students create a "Hall Bulletin Board." The students find a picture in a magazine that looks like them, draw a picture of themselves, or you take a picture of every child. The pictures can be placed on a poster, mural, or collage in the hall. Above their picture, the students can make a hat and write their name on it. The bulletin board is entitled "The Fourth Grade Class Is Here "or "The Brady (teacher's name) Bunch Says Hello" or "Hats Off to This Year."

END-OF-THE-DAY ROUTINE: Pass out a "Rewards Survey." The students will take about five minutes and complete the following sentences.

1. Rewards are _____
2. I think rewards are important because_____
3. I deserve a reward when _____
4. Rewards I would like to have are_____
5. I do not deserve a reward when _____
6. Another word for reward is _____

Place the surveys in the students' Performance Portfolios. For younger students, take one sentence, discuss it with them, and write the words they want to use to complete the sentence. The students read the sentence together or copy it.

REMINDERS:
- ✔ Remember "Funny Box" or "What's Up" box.
- ✔ Remember "Marble Jar."
- ✔ Remember colored index cards for "Unstuck Procedure."
- ✔ Prepare survey strips—long strips of white paper—with the students' response to the survey.
- ✔ Prepare name cards of faculty and staff members.
- ✔ Continue to call about five students each night to say hello and to give the date of the "Open House" and to ask for their support for a great year.

DAY 2—I BELIEVE IN ME

BEGIN THE DAY: Teacher and student greeter meet the students in the morning.

ROUTINE PROCEDURE: The routine procedure every morning is for the students to first get prepared for class upon entering the room and then to write in their journals for ten minutes. Continue to monitor and reinforce.

USE CUE: Raise your hand and move to the front of the room.

GUIDELINES: Discuss the interest survey information by reporting the class statistics. Get statistics for majority responses. Do a "Get Acquainted" activity. Prepare survey strips by writing each student response on a strip of paper. Allow students to select a strip and try to name the person who made the response. Also include a teacher survey strip. Survey strips can say things such as, "Pizza is my favorite food," "I like to ride my bike," "I play baseball," "I love my Nintendo," or "I take gymnastics."

ACTIVITY: The object of this activity is to introduce the students to other faculty and staff members (principals, librarian, secretary, nurse, janitor, other teachers). Have students find their buddy. Prepare name cards of faculty and staff and assign each buddy pair to a person to interview. In this "Think, Pair, and Share" activity, the pair will work together to develop five interview questions. Students need to make an appointment to interview this person. The appointments are to made sometime during the month of September. You will have alerted the staff and faculty of this project. The students can share their interview information with the class. The students need to arrange a time with you to share this information.

For younger students, arrange to have staff and faculty people come to the classroom and tell students a little about themselves and their jobs. Encourage the students to ask them questions.

AFTER-LUNCH ROUTINE: SSR time

PLANNED LESSONS AND ACTIVITIES

Use the established cue to gain everyone's attention. Continue to teach student accountability.

- **Topic**—5-Step Unstuck Procedure (Bosch & Kersey 1993).
- **Opener**—Present students with the following scenario: A student is having a problem with an assignment that a teacher has just given. The assignment needs to be turned in by the end of the class. The student has several choices. What are they?

    List the students' choices on the board. Ask several students what they would choose to do? Why?
- **Objectives**—The student will be able to:
    1. list three reasons why problem solvers are needed.
    2. outline the 5-Step Unstuck Procedure.
    3. use the 5-Step Unstuck Procedure.
- **Instruction**—Lead a discussion in the importance of problem solving? Why do we need to solve problems? Does it help the student? Does it help the teacher?

    Present three reasons on the board or on a transparency. A transparency reveals a problem solver called the "unstuck procedure." Discuss each step of the "5-Step Unstuck Procedure" (Bosch & Kersey 1993) and ask for examples. The steps are as follows:
    1. Reread the directions.
    2. Go on to the next problem or item. Then go back and complete as much as you can.
    3. Ask the peer assistant for help.
    4. Place a colored index card (signal) on your desk for assistance from the teacher.
    5. Take out a book to read. *(Reprinted with permission of the Helen Dwight Reid Educational Foundation. Published by Heldref Publications, 1319 18th Street, N.W. Washington, D.C. 20036-18020. Copyright 1993.)*

    Discuss the use of the colored index card. Give everyone an index card to use for assistance. The red card means the student needs help from the teacher. Have the students copy the "5-Step Unstuck Procedure" and put it in the Performance Portfolios. Place a poster of the "5-Step Unstuck Procedure" on the front board or wall for the class to use.

- **Guided Practice**—Provide scenarios of student problems. Give some steps taken and omit some steps that should have been taken. Ask students to write down the missing step(s).
- **Closure**—Give me one reason the "5-Step Unstuck Procedure" is important? Give me the first step? second step?
- **Independent Practice**—Give older students written scenarios of a student with a problem that can be solved by using the "5-Step Unstuck Procedure." Have the students finish this assignment and collect.

END-OF-THE-DAY ROUTINE: Give the students some sample situations needing correction and ask them, "What is our correction plan?" Situations may be presented for incentives as well. Call out an appropriate or inappropriate behavior and ask for the consequence or incentive to be given. Drop marbles in the jar or add a letter(s) to the secret word if class has learned the management plan.

REMINDERS:
- ✔ Use the "Funny Box" or "What's Up" box.
- ✔ Use the "Marble Jar."
- ✔ Begin to document behaviors—attempt to identify the most difficult times or activities.

DAY 3—I WILL SURVIVE—I WILL SUCCEED

BEGIN THE DAY: Teacher and student greeter meet the students in the morning.

ROUTINE PROCEDURE: The routine procedure every morning is for the students to first get prepared for class upon entering the room and then to write in their journals for ten minutes.

USE CUE: Raise your hand and move to the front of the room. Continue to monitor amount of time it takes to get everyone's attention.

ACTIVITY: Continue to build positive peer relationships. Have each student draw a name from a hat. Use name cards from the first week. Beneath the name the student writes a positive word (adjective) to describe the student. The name cards are placed on the students' backs. Each student may ask another student three questions that can be answered with a yes or no response. The object is for the students to guess the word written about them.

AFTER-LUNCH ROUTINE: Read aloud to students.

PLANNED LESSONS AND ACTIVITIES

Use the established cue to gain everyone's attention.

- **Topic**—Group Cohesiveness
- **Opener**—Show the students a picture. Ask them to look for similarities. Discuss what they have in common, what they share. Ask two students to come to the front of the room. Ask students how are these students alike. How many have the same color eyes? How many ride the same bus?

  For younger students, you will have to find group or class similarities. For example, name things (animals) and have everyone who likes that thing stand up. The class begins to see that they are alike.

- **Objectives**—The student will be able to:
  1. discover similarities among individuals in the class.
  2. examine the similarities of the class as a whole.

- **Instruction**—Assign the students to teams (an odd number in each team) and begin working on answering the questions below. The team must answer each question. In other words, they must take the answer said by most members of the team as the team answer to the question. These team answers will be shared and discussed.
  1. What is the group's favorite color?
  2. What is the group's favorite school subject?
  3. What is the group's favorite sport?
  4. What is the group's favorite television program?
  5. What is the group's special learning interest?

  Continue to examine the similarities of the class as a whole. What similarities are shared by the teams? What similarities are shared by all of the teams?

- **Closure**—What have we learned from this activity?

  We have many similarities and we share many things. We have this class in common and this teacher. We will be sharing this learning space for the school year. We need to work and learn together.

END-OF-THE-DAY ROUTINE: Say to students: "Tell me what you can do when you get stuck on an assignment?"

REMINDERS:
- ✔ Use "Marble Jar."
- ✔ Begin planning learning centers.

DAY 4 —USE THE WORDS *WE, OUR,* AND *US* . . . .

BEGIN THE DAY: Teacher and student greeter meet the students in the morning.

ROUTINE PROCEDURE: The routine procedure every morning is for the students to first get prepared for class upon entering the room and then to write in their journals for ten minutes.

USE CUE: Raise your hand and move to the front of the room.

GUIDELINES: The theme for this month is "Freedom." Discuss how this theme can be developed. The class will develop themes for the months. This can be accomplished by brainstorming as a whole group activity. Brainstorm one month at a time or for the ten months. A small group activity can be to break the class into small groups (four members) to think of themes. Each group presents ideas and places them on the board. The class will vote on a theme for this month or themes of the months. The class plans ways to reinforce the theme(s). For younger students, the themes are given and the students can plan class activities.

AFTER-LUNCH ROUTINE: SSR time

PLANNED LESSONS AND ACTIVITIES
. . . .

Use the established cue to gain everyone's attention. The teacher plans more get-acquainted lessons and activities.
- **Topic**—Getting to Know You
- **Opener**—Present a time line of your life. Ask the students to read the events and dates from the time line. Guess whose time line this is?
- **Objectives**—The student will be able to:
  1. identify items found on a time line.
  2. construct a time line.

3. create a time line of one's life.
- **Instruction**—Present several time lines containing information and show the development of a time line (chronologically). Have students list items found on time lines. As a class, do a time line together from a prepared list of items.
- **Guided Practice**—Have students construct a time line at their seats using a prepared list of items. Monitor the activity. If students can handle the information, you can proceed to the second objective. If the students are having difficulty, do another example together and have them construct another time line at their seats.
- **Closure**—What does a time line tell us about a person? What kinds of things are placed on time lines?
- **Independent Practice**—Tell students: "Write down the key items you want to appear on your time line. Construct a time line of your life and place these items on it." Older students can predict what their time lines might include in the future. When the students are finished, have them put their name at the top of their paper and place the time line on the back bulletin board. Have younger students construct a time line of their life with their parents' help.

END-OF-THE-DAY ROUTINE: For closure, model the cues used and asks students what they mean and how are they to respond.

REMINDERS:
- ✔ Select computer software to supplement curriculum.
- ✔ Set up learning centers.
- ✔ Prepare "Leap Into Learning Together" poster.
- ✔ Prepare "Class Meeting Agenda" poster.

DAY 5—DEMONSTRATE "WITH-IT-NESS"

BEGIN THE DAY: Teacher and student greeter meet the students in the morning.

ROUTINE PROCEDURE: The routine procedure every morning is for the students to first get prepared for class upon entering the room and then to write in their journals for ten minutes. Continue to monitor and review.

USE CUE: Raise your hand and move to the front of the room.

GUIDELINES: Discuss with the students ways to increase success with cooperative learning. Ask: "How can we be successful in working together and learning together?" Set up a T-graph and list ways to be successful and ways that interfere with success. Present "LEAP into Learning Together" rules for cooperative groups to be successful:

> Listen to each member.
> Encourage each other to participate.
> Accept each member's ideas.
> Praise the thoughts/ideas/work of each member.

Discuss what each letter means and how that can work in a group.

ACTIVITY: Introduce the learning centers that are set up in the room. Discuss the reasons for the learning centers. Remind the students that the following procedures are needed as well as the class rules when using the learning centers. Discuss when learning centers are to be used. They can be used if you finish your assigned work, during your free time, and if you come in early or decide to stay late. The learning centers are also assigned weekly as part of a rotation of activities to be completed by the class, groups, and individuals. The learning center procedures are as follows:

1. Four students can work at each learning center. (Determine a maximum number of students that can work at a learning center at a time.)
2. What you begin, you must finish.
3. Put all materials back where they belong when you are finished.

AFTER-LUNCH ROUTINE: Read aloud to the students.

PLANNED LESSONS AND ACTIVITIES

Use the established cue to gain everyone's attention. Begin to prepare students for the class meeting to be held the third Friday of every month.
- **Topic**—Class Meeting
- **Opener**—Class discussion on students' rights. Say: "What rights in this class are important to you? Rights are important. They are freedoms and they are responsibilities. How can we as a class protect and preserve our rights? What are the different forums we can use to protect our rights? Let's plan a democratic process that can serve us. A class meeting is such a process. It provides us with a forum, a desig-

nated time, and an amount of time to recognize accomplishments and discuss difficulties, solve problems, and make changes."

- **Objectives**—The student will be able to:
1. describe a class meeting.
2. examine the value of class meetings.
- **Instruction**—Teach the concept of the class meeting. It is an opportunity to discuss things they like about the class as well as things they may need to change in order for the class to run smoothly. For older students, introduce the agenda for a class meetings.

   A. Class Meeting
   1. Call to Order.
   2. Minutes Taken.
   3. Daily Items Read.
   B. Accomplishments Recognized
   C. Difficulties Reported
   D. Problem Solvers
   1. State Problem.
   2. Brainstorm Solutions.
   3. Choose a Solution.
   4. Vote on Solution.
   E. Adjourn Class Meeting

   The class meeting needs to follow a format. No agenda; no class meeting. If a student has an item to place on the agenda, the item is listed on the poster entitled "Class Meeting Agenda". The teacher must put up a new poster each month. Remember to stress that a class meeting is not a gripe session. Tell them: "Each month, on the third Friday, we will have our class meeting. That is the time we will share what works and what is not working in our class. We suggest changes and take it to majority vote. If something important needs to be discussed immediately, we can schedule a special session."

- **Guided Practice**—Have the students copy the agenda and take notes from the discussion and place it in their Performance Portfolios in order to refer to it if needed.
- **Closure**—Our first class meeting is tomorrow. It will give us an opportunity to see how we can make this activity work for our class.
- **Independent Practice**—Prepare an assignment with true/false statements about freedom and rights. Have the students answer these statements and explain their answers. When students complete the assignment, have them place it in the "In" basket. The assignment will be returned to students tomorrow to discuss and then placed in their Performance Portfolios.

_____ 1. Freedom is a responsibility.

Explanation _____

_____ 2. Freedom allows me to change things.

Explanation _____

_____ 3. Freedom gives me choices.

Explanation _____

_____ 4. Freedom is for all people.

Explanation _____

_____ 5. Freedom is doing anything I want.

Explanation _____

_____ 6. Freedom is class meetings.

Explanation _____

_____7. Freedom is the right to learn without someone interfering with my learning.

Explanation _____

For younger students, take one sentence, discuss it, and write it the way they want to complete it, and read it together or copy it. They can draw a picture or color one to represent the topic.

GUIDELINES: Select a student to be the computer trainer to assist student(s) working on the computer. Allow the student to take software home to preview and become familiar with the program. The computer trainer is to make a class banner (class name) using the computer and display it on the wall.

END-OF-THE-DAY ROUTINE: Say to students: "Tell me one thing you learned today."

REMINDERS:
- ✔ Remember "Funny Box."
- ✔ Remember the "Marble Jar."
- ✔ Select a new student greeter.
- ✔ Prepare Bloom's Taxonomy chart.

FOURTH WEEK

GOAL: MONITOR AND CORRECT WHAT IS IMPORTANT

Key Teaching Areas:
- ❑ Enforce Management Plan and PPSP.
- ❑ Strengthen Group Cohesiveness.
- ❑ Develop Class Unity and Spirit.
- ❑ Build Positive Peer Pressure.
- ❑ Develop Class Newsletter.

Success Strategies:
- ❑ Use Cooperative Learning.
- ❑ Practice With-it-ness.
- ❑ Stop, Go Back, Correct, and Enforce Management Plan.

DAY 1—BE A FACILITATOR

BEGIN THE DAY: Teacher and student greeter meet the students in the morning.

ROUTINE PROCEDURE: The routine procedure every morning is for the students to first get prepared for class upon entering the room and then to write in their journals for ten minutes.

USE CUE: Raise your hand and move to the front of the room. Continue to monitor the amount of time it takes to get everyone's attention. If students take too much time, take time from students to reinforce this procedure.

GUIDELINES: Share with students a special class project planned by the teacher: selecting students each month to read to younger students or classes, or preparing materials for the school foyer bulletin board. Select two or more students to begin the class project. Allow them to go to the teacher who is participating and set up a time and place to begin this activity.

PLANNED LESSONS AND ACTIVITIES

Use the established cue to gain everyone's attention. Introduce Bloom's

Taxonomy to the students.

- **Topic**—Bloom's Taxonomy
- **Opener**—Ask students a question that requires a factual answer. Ask them a question that requires an answer of "Yes" or "No." Ask them a third question that is an opinion question that can have many answers. Let the students think for a minute about the three questions. Which question was different and why?
- **Objectives**—The student will be able to:
  1. identify the six levels of Bloom's Taxonomy (knowledge, comprehension, application, analysis, synthesis, and evaluation).
  2. develop questions using Bloom's Taxonomy.
- **Instruction**—Prepare a poster of Bloom's Taxonomy to be posted in the room for use by the students. The students will be given the levels, sample questions, and verbs to use at the various levels. (A discussion of the six levels can be found in Bloom, 1956.) The students are required to take notes. Ask a few questions and have the students identify the level of the taxonomy. Explain to the students that the higher level questions come from the analysis, synthesis, and evaluation domains. Critical thinking skills are developed through the use of these domains.
- **Guided Practice**—For older students, plan a cooperative learning activity. Go through the "Guidelines for Giving Directions" and assign students to groups of six. Have each group read a short article and develop questions from the six levels. Assign a level to each student in the group (six students per group and six levels) and he or she is responsible for developing a question based on the article. Together they put the six questions from the six levels of Bloom's Taxonomy on a sheet of paper to be handed in to the teacher. The members of the group sign their names to the sheet.
- **Closure**—Why is Bloom's Taxonomy important to know and use? Why should questioning come from all levels of the Taxonomy? Who can make up a question from the application domain?

AFTER-LUNCH ROUTINE: SSR time

ACTIVITY: Explain to the students that the class meeting is scheduled for today. Approximately 45 minutes are budgeted. The students need to follow the procedures and agenda established. The students will be looking at the management plan. Ask such questions as, Are the rules effective? Are they being followed? How are the correction procedures working? Do you all feel informed? If something is not working, what do we as a class do about it? When do we present the information? How do we go about being heard?

If the class meeting does not go as planned, stop the meeting, and discuss what is happening. Get both student involvement and assistance by asking students what is wrong with the meeting and what is needed to improve the process. Expect appropriate behavior and student accountability. Assist certain students to move toward more self-discipline as well as group accountability. A class norm for behavior and achievement is developed, nurtured, and enforced. Remain consistent in getting students to discuss, correct, and maintain a positive learning environment.

END-OF-THE-DAY ROUTINE: For closure, pass back to the students the freedom and rights assignment. The students can discuss and place the assignment in their performance portfolios.

REMINDERS:
   ✔ Make Suggestion/Dialogue Box.

DAY 2—PRACTICE "WITH-IT-NESS" ● ● ● ● ● ● ● ● ● ● ● ● ● ● ●

BEGIN THE DAY: Teacher and student greeter meet the students in the morning.

ROUTINE PROCEDURE: The routine procedure every morning is for the students to first get prepared for class upon entering the room and then to write in their journals for ten minutes.

USE CUE: Raise your hand and move to the front of the room.

GUIDELINES: Developing a suggestion/dialogue box is another important part of the first few weeks. The suggestion/dialogue box has several purposes. It can be used for suggestions to improve the learning environment and the amount of student learning. It is also a way for the teacher and a student to "talk" confidentially to one another.

A "Talk Time" may be introduced to further the relationship building between students and teacher. The "Talk Time" can be scheduled based on need. It can be a whole group activity, a small group activity, or a one-on-one conference time.

AFTER-LUNCH ROUTINE: Begin reading newspapers—current events—to the class.

ACTIVITY: Prepare students for writing a class newsletter. This activity will reinforce positive peer relationships and group cohesiveness and will develop class unity and spirit by providing a situation for students to work and learn together on a class project. A newsletter also provides a direct link to the parents. It is essential to keep the parents informed and interested in what is going on in the classroom.

A class newsletter is prepared on a monthly (quarterly) basis to inform the parents and other interested persons on what is going on in the classroom as reported by the students. Develop the idea of a newsletter by getting student input on topics to be included. Design a name and logo for newsletter. Review several newsletters and decide what to include in the first newsletter. Use a production date of the first of every month.

Have the committees get together to develop the text. The planned lessons each month include the following:

> First meeting—develop text.
> Second meeting—share text and agree.
> Third meeting—edit material.
> Fourth meeting—ready for publication, discuss future copies, additional coverage, and extra features.

Use the computer to produce this newsletter. Examples of appropriate software are the Children's Writing & Publishing Center (from The Learning Company), Newsroom (from Scholastic), and Print Shop (from Broderbund).

For younger students, the newsletter is a teacher-directed activity. It can be done in a weekly class period or two. Some suggestions for content are the following: names of everyone in the class, unfinished sentences such as "I like my class because..." or "My favorite animal is...," and writing sentences together about things they have learned. You can put the information into the computer with the students watching you and give them a chance to type in their names next to the sentences, and so on. Additional information can be included to alert the parents to upcoming events. Teachers have commented that the newsletter always makes it home; where as teacher written notices or handouts seldom reach their proper destination.

END-OF-THE-DAY ROUTINE: For closure, ask sudents: "What is class spirit? What are our class projects? What do you like best about this class?"

REMINDERS:
✔ Remember "Funny Box" or "What's Up" box.
✔ Remember "Marble Jar."
✔ Begin peer tutoring.
✔ Prepare application forms for peer tutors.

DAY 3—BE PROACTIVE NOT REACTIVE

BEGIN THE DAY: Teacher and student greeter meet the students in the morning.

ROUTINE PROCEDURE: The routine procedure every morning is for the students to first get prepared for class upon entering the room and then to write in their journals for ten minutes. Continue to monitor.

USE CUE: Raise your hand and move to the front of the room.

AFTER-LUNCH ROUTINE: Pass out newspapers and have the students silently read an article and discuss why they liked the article and if it was easy to read. Prepare students for the after-lunch routine on Friday in which the students will read a short article from a newspaper or magazine and tell the class why they liked the article.

PLANNED LESSONS AND ACTIVITIES

Use the established cue to gain everyone's attention.
- **Topic**—Prepare Students for Writing a Newsletter
- **Opener**—Discuss with students the idea of a class newsletter. Put the word newsletter in a word cloud and brainstorm what areas could be covered in the newsletter.
- **Objectives**—The student will be able to:
  1. identify areas for the newsletter.
  2. develop job tasks for committees.
- **Instruction**—Areas that need to be covered include math, language arts, science, and social studies and other areas of interest, announcements, future projects, activities, and so on. You must remind the students that the newsletter should be written in a quality way and that students take on the role of a reporter. Everyone is to be involved and all names are included in every issue. Have students take notes and begin thinking of what is included under each area and begin to move toward a number of committees with a specific focus (committee for science, committee for special interests) and certain tasks that must be completed. Agree on a number of committees and ask the students to choose a reporter on the six o'clock news to follow as we look at the role of reporting. (The students are assigned committees by topic with the teacher making such selections based on data from interest survey and participation in the get acquainted activities.)

> • **Closure**—Tell me the areas chosen for the newsletter. What are some of the tasks developed for the committees?

END-OF-THE-DAY ROUTINE: Ask the students: "How does the management plan (rules, correction, incentives) give you freedom?"

REMINDERS:
- ✔ Remember "Marble Jar."
- ✔ Select peer tutors for the month.
- ✔ Select tutors from applications.
- ✔ Plan peer tutor training.

DAY 4—BE HAPPY, DON'T WORRY

BEGIN THE DAY: Teacher and student greeter meet the students in the morning.

ROUTINE PROCEDURE: The routine procedure every morning is for the students to first get prepared for class upon entering the room and then to write in their journals for ten minutes.

USE CUE: Raise your hand and move to the front of the room. Continue to monitor the amount of time it takes to get everyone's attention. Reward or reinforce this procedure

AFTER-LUNCH ROUTINE: Read aloud a newspaper article. After reading, tell the students why you liked the article. This should prepare students for Friday when they are to read newspaper articles and tell the class why they liked them.

ACTIVITY: Continue to prepare students for the writing of the newsletter. Prepare a poster with each committee and the tasks to be completed in groups. Review the "Guidelines for Giving Directions" and "LEAP into Learning Together" rules and direct the students through the procedure. Assign members to committees to develop a rough draft. Each group places a rough draft in the file under the bulletin board entitled "Our Class Newsletter." A colored piece of paper is circulated listing the committees and the members sign their name under their committee. This is placed on the bulletin board. Newsletters, as they are completed, will be placed on this bulletin board.

END-OF-THE-DAY ROUTINE: Say to students: "Tell me something you would like to learn more about. Tell me something you learned today in math. English."

REMINDERS:
  ✔ Remember "Funny Box" or "What's Up" box.
  ✔ Remember "Marble Jar."

DAY 5—I BELIEVE THE CHILDREN ARE OUR FUTURE

BEGIN THE DAY: Teacher and student greeter meet the students in the morning.

ROUTINE PROCEDURE: The routine procedure every morning is for the students to first get prepared for class upon entering the room and then to write in their journals for ten minutes.

USE CUE: Raise your hand and move to the front of the room.

GUIDELINES: Discuss the role of a peer tutor. Show students the form to apply for the position. Discuss the job description, qualities needed, and requirements. (Select peer tutors from applications and prepare this process for October. Remind students under "Guidelines" to fill out applications. Plan an after school training session for peer tutors).

ACTIVITY: Review the "Guidelines for Giving Directions" and have the committees once again edit the rough draft of the newsletter. Have the students share the articles with the class and get final approval of the newsletter.

AFTER-LUNCH ROUTINE: SSR time reading newspapers and magazine articles.

GUIDELINES: Discuss special days with the class. The class can plan a Yellow Day (students wear yellow and work on yellow paper); Sports Day (wear something related to sports); and Twin Day (wear matching clothes and work in pairs).

END-OF-THE-DAY ROUTINE: For closure, ask the students: "If someone new came to our class, what information can you share with him or her about our class? Which class member is responsible for new students?"

REMINDERS:
  ✔ Remember to use "Funny Box."
  ✔ Remember to use "Marble Jar."

✔ Assign student greeter.

Continue the management plan into the second month. See that the format continues and new ideas are inserted. Additional ideas are presented for possible inclusion into the management plan at a later date.

END OF THE FIRST MONTH

This ends the first month. Each month, you need to review what is being done, prepare for certain routine activities, make certain assignments, and begin presenting new ideas. You must make a list of the reminders as well as needed supplies for continuing the management plan. A partial list for maintaining the operation has been started for you along with some new ideas.

REMINDERS:
   ✔ Prepare assignment sheet and/or calendar.
   ✔ Use peer tutors and assign a peer tutor for November.
   ✔ Use computer tutors and assign a computer tutor for November.
   ✔ Use the established cue to gain everyone's attention for teaching a lesson.
   ✔ Remember the class meeting on the third Friday of the month.
   ✔ Remember "Funny Box" and "Marble Jar."
   ✔ Remember class projects: reading to students, bulletin board, and the newsletter.
   ✔ Remember newsletter development during a month:

      First meeting—develop text.
      Second meeting—share text and agree.
      Third meeting—edit material.
      Fourth meeting—ready for publication and discuss future copies, additional coverage, and extra features.

   ✔ Plan to have past tutors train new tutors one day after school.

More ideas for possible inclusion in the management plan in the months to follow are:

   ✔ "Teacher Help" sessions.
   ✔ Student Teaching Day—The students will be given the opportunity to teach the class a lesson. The students will be given the topic to teach

and have fifteen minutes to teach it. The topic will support your planned lessons.

✔ Teach the Lesson Plan Outline (see Figure 3). Share the outline with the students and discuss what it means to the teacher and to the students. Highlight roles of the teacher and the student in learning. It is important to demonstrate accountability to the teaching/learning process as well as to establish a sense of ownership, responsibility, control, and power for one's own learning. The format includes the following: Topic, Opener, Objectives, Instruction (check for understanding and guided practice), Closure, Independent Practice, and Evaluation.

III. COMMENTS FROM FIRST-YEAR TEACHERS

The management plan was field tested by 25 first-year teachers. Their feedback was incorporated into this plan. Some of the comments of these first-year teachers have been included to provide yet another way to meet the first-year teachers' needs and concerns.

> Kim (5th grade): My first week has been absolutely fantastic. I taught the rules the first week and next my cue. My cue is to raise my hand, they look at me, raise their hand, and close their mouths. It works in the room, in line, in the hallway, and even in the gym. The most amazing thing to me is that they try to quiet each other down and when I'm walking to the front of the room, they are already raising their hands.

> Joan (6th grade class): My students loved the puzzle activity. I used puzzle glue and displayed the puzzle in the classroom. When we are not working together, I refer to the puzzle and we discuss it.

> The management plan must work because one girl at the end of the day said, "I don't feel like I"m going to throwup today. I know how this class is going to work." After further discussion, she revealed that she always feels sick the first day of school.

> I always use the cue to begin instruction. The cue I have chosen is to walk to the front of the room and hold up the book

or homework folder of the next subject. I time the response with a stopwatch and place the amount of time taken on the chalkboard. No reward is attached; students just like to get a good time.

Imelda (5th grade): There are not enough corners in the room so correction isn't enough; a management plan is essential.

Kelly (4/5th grade): This management plan works! We practiced and I reviewed and retaught the plan. For example, walking down the hall correctly was a real challenge. We walked poorly the first day. I stopped the class and made them return to the class and we walked the hallway with appropriate and expected behavior. My expectations were high and I consistently reviewed and enforced. Then the veteran teachers in my building were telling me that I didn't look or act like a first-year teacher. They were saying things like, "You are in control," and "You follow through." Words like these are great for a first-year teacher's ego, confidence, and for your bad days. Many teachers in my building wanted to see this management plan and get a copy of it. My principal mentioned that he would like all of his teachers in his school using this plan.

Cynthia (5th grade): The plan gave me the confidence I needed. I knew what to do. I looked good!

Lisa (7th grade): My team member and I were called the "Mighty Mites" by our principal. We both are short in stature, but we were very much in control. We followed the management plan and felt we were together in philosophy, expectations, and operation. The consistency was empowering.

Diane (3rd grade): This is my second year of teaching. The first year, I did not have a management plan and I took the "Wimp" approach. I did what the other teachers told me to do for rules and discipline as I certainly did not want to alienate them. I was not happy and extremely inconsistent. This year, with the plan, I have a guide and directions for putting together my real first year of teaching—my way!

Jennifer (Kindergarten): I was worried about knowing what and how to do what is needed. You get the books and materials for the academic part of teaching, but you can't teach without managing. The management plan helped me pull it all together. I like my start.

The pilot group admitted they felt the pressure as first-year teachers to teach less management and push academics immediately. They expressed concern about keeping up with the rest of the teachers and being on the same pages if not ahead. To accommodate this need and concern, the authors suggest that the management plan be spread out over a longer period of time and not just stopped because of lack of time or pressure to move through the curriculum. The first-year teacher must realize the first one or two chapters of the textbooks are designed to be review. This should afford you the time to concentrate on management. When the pressure is present to be on the same pages, one might plan to gain pages by truly reviewing and not requiring that each page, all the problems, activities, and exercises be done by the students. Teaching your management plan will result in a true readiness for teaching academics.

The overall responses to the management plan were positive. The first-year teachers involved in the field-based study agreed that they felt prepared to teach the curriculum. They felt that they knew how to write lesson plans and had some experience teaching students and being in classrooms. The schools gave them textbooks, manuals, and curriculum guides to direct their efforts in teaching but nothing to help them with management. They all agreed that the management plan gave them the needed direction and confidence in managing student behavior, student learning, and the day-to-day operation of the classroom. The first-year teachers reported that they now know how to take control, how to be in control, and how to plan for such control. This book and management plan provide assistance, affirmation, and assurance that a teacher can be effective and students can be successful.

CHAPTER 3:

HOW DO I WORK WITH PARENTS?

I. RELATIONSHIP BUILDING

The evidence is beyond dispute: Students do better in school when their parents are involved in their education! In schools where parents are involved, Henderson (1987) finds:

- ✔ higher test scores and grades.
- ✔ more positive behavior.
- ✔ more positive attitudes.
- ✔ more long-term academic achievement.
- ✔ more successful programs.
- ✔ more effective schools.

In his study of American schools, James Coleman (Henderson 1987) found that students who go to private and Catholic schools perform better than those who attend public schools. They make better grades and test scores, they are more likely to stay in school, and they are more likely to attend and graduate from college. This can not be explained away by selective admission practices, because Catholic schools serve populations—including those from disadvantaged backgrounds—comparable to public schools.

Why, then? Coleman concluded that the one outstanding characteristic common to these private schools was that of parental involvement—active participation of parents in the learning process. When children are aware that their teachers and parents know each other, work together for common goals, form meaningful attachments on their behalf, and share mutual ownership for their school success, they will assume the responsibility necessary to work to their potential. In other words, when there is a continuous flow of communication between home and school, the child's educational experience is greatly enhanced.

Many parents are reluctant to get involved in the classroom. In an effort to alert parents to their worth in the classroom—beyond the usual housekeeping, parties, and clerical work—the administration of the UCLA laboratory school (Hunter 1989) identified three possible categories of competencies:

1. skills in hobbies and crafts;
2. direct knowledge and experience in occupations;
3. appreciation of, knowledge of, or skills in many aspects of different cultures.

Then they invited parents to a two-hour inservice session, where teachers demonstrated effective teaching techniques and illustrated ways to make lessons successful. Care was also taken to help parents develop a sensitivity to issues of privacy and confidentiality, so that they would adopt professional precautions to protect children and their families. The results were overwhelmingly successsful. The parents who were willing to involve themselves in this process were more willing to take active roles in their children's education, and the teachers reported improvement in their children's academic performance.

Jennings (1989) found that most parents have the ability, energy, and talent to play all roles at school, including that of decision-maker. In those schools where parents are invited to become involved in higher level decisions, there is more creativity, resourcefulness, and ingenuity being displayed. In fact, when they are challenged to contribute their energy and ideas, there are significant changes being made toward educational progress and resource allocations. Furthermore, the more parents represented at the decision-making table, the less finger-pointing and blaming occurs, and the more shared responsibility and respect are modeled in the community.

Children of all ages need for their parents to take an active interest and place in the school. It is easy for parents to underestimate their importance to the child. Often when children become adolescents, parents feel that they should "back off," for fear that their children will think they are overbearing, or that the school will think they are overprotective. Actually, children of this age need their parents to stay involved. Although outwardly they may seem nonchalant or callous, inwardly they very much need caring parents who will help them as they charter the frightening seas to adulthood (Berla 1992).

Therefore, it is absolutely essential that parents and teachers sign up on the same team with the child. If either pulls against the other, or undermines the other, or belittles or criticizes the other, the effect will be lower performance on the part of the child.

If the benefit of working together is so obvious, why is it so difficult to achieve? Some of the answer lies in our history. Some of us recall bad experiences from the past that consciously or unconsciously affect our present notions. More of the answer lies in our own feelings of inadequacy. Because we are human, we shy away from encounters that may become confrontational or unpleasant, or where we may be put on the defensive.

Below are listed many of the obstacles to parent involvement— possible reasons why parents and teachers may feel uncomfortable working together. Since we, the authors, are both parents and have taught in the classroom, we can see the problem from both points of view. We strongly believe that when teachers and parents can see that both parties feel vulnerable and at times unsure and nervous, each will be willing to put forth the extra effort it takes to WORK TOGETHER on behalf of the child.

TEACHER FEARS ABOUT PARENTS

Teachers are unsure of the role parents want to play in the classroom. In workshops we have conducted for teachers, many teachers have concerns over the parents' motives; others felt hopeless, expressing their concern that the dynamics between the two groups were such that each would always be suspicious of the other. Below are lists of the fears that teachers have expressed about parents and that parents have expressed about teachers:

1. Parents may only want to volunteer in their child's class, which may create problems for the child or the teacher.
2. A parent may take too much responsibility in the class without checking with the teacher first.
3. Parents may try to handle discipline problems themselves instead of consulting the teacher.
4. A parent may give incorrect information when tutoring or do the work for the child instead of encouraging the child to do his or her own work.
5. A parent may make judgments about a teacher's ability to handle the class.
6. A parent may lack the skills necessary to work with children.
7. There may be a lack of communication between parent and teacher.
8. A parent may break the confidentiality of the classroom by talking to other parents about a particular child's behavior or situation.
9. A parent's presence may cause behavior problems with his or her child.
10. The teacher may feel that limited class time would be more effectively used by a professional educator.
11. A parent may be a poor role model.
12. A parent may be excessively harsh with his or her own child or with other students.

13. The teacher may feel pressured to give special consideration to the parent's child while the parent is there.
14. The teacher may lack the patience to train the parent or may be reluctant to do the extra planning required to keep the parent involved.
15. The teacher may feel apprehensive because of a previous experience with another parent.
16. The teacher may have little support if the principal or other members of school administration feel negatively about parental involvement.
17. A parent may show favoritism, focused only on his or her own child, or, on the other hand, may ignore his or her child, overcompensating in an effort to be fair.
18. A parent might create problems with other parents if he or she criticizes the teacher's methods to them.
19. A parent may become "overinvolved," always dropping in unexpectedly or demanding too much of the teacher's time.
20. Teachers may feel that they will be unable to rely on parents to show up when scheduled.
21. A child may be embarrassed or uncomfortable about his or her parent's involvement in the class.
22. The teacher and the parent may both feel uncertain as to who should discipline if the parent's child misbehaves.
23. The teacher may worry that by having parents assist him or her, it will appear that he or she is unable to do the job.
24. The teacher may fear that students will like the parent better than him or her.

PARENT FEARS ABOUT TEACHERS

Parents may feel uneasy about talking with teachers, let alone spending time in the classroom. The following issues are real fears that are felt by many parents, as evidenced in workshops for parents (Kersey 1990), and they must be considered when reaching out to parents.

1. Parents may fear that the teacher will judge them or label them as "bad parents."
2. Parents may be intimidated by the terminology that the teacher uses.
3. Parents may resent the authority figure that a teacher represents.
4. Parents may make false assumptions about the teacher based on what their

child has told them.

5. Parents may fear that if they are too assertive, the teacher may not like them and take it out on their child.
6. Parents may fear that the teacher will gossip about them or their child to other teachers.
7. Parents may feel as if the teacher is taking over the parental role and they may feel threatened by that.
8. Parents may fear teachers due to their own negative experiences in school.
9. Parents may feel inferior to the teacher because of his or her degrees.
10. Parents may fear that the teacher will blame them for their child's behavior in school.
11. Parents may feel that the teacher is merely doing a job and has no real concern for their child.
12. Parents may not want to hear that their child is having problems, fearing that they will be powerless to change whatever is causing the problem.
13. Parents may fear the unknown of the school system and procedures.
14. Parents may fear that they will be misunderstood or not listened to by the teacher.
15. Parents may feel that the school system does not understand their needs or those of their child.
16. Parents may feel guilty that they didn't take time to help their child.
17. Parents may have had learning problems themselves and be embarrassed if their child does, too.
18. Parents may fear exposing too much about the home situation or their own personality.
19. Parents may feel intimidated by socioeconomic differences between themselves and the teacher.
20. Parents may fear that the teacher will be unwilling to listen to their ideas and concerns.
21. Parents may have much of their self-esteem invested in their child's success and therefore wish to avoid the teacher if there is a chance he or she may tell them something negative about their child.
22. Parents may fear that the teacher will compare their child negatively to other children.
23. Parents may feel that the teacher knows more about them than they want him or her to know.
24. Parents and teachers may differ in their opinions of appropriate classroom behavior.

II. EFFECTIVE COMMUNICATION

The best time for parents and teachers to get to know each other is before problems arise. Parents and teachers have unique, yet overlapping roles. A parent's role is to love each child so that he or she feels validated as an individual human being. The teacher's role is to love and validate a classroom full of individual human beings.

Communication is the most important skill for a teacher. No matter how prepared a teacher is, no matter how experienced or well trained, if a teacher cannot communicate effectively with children and parents, he or she will not be successful in the classroom. Therefore, we feel that it is essential for first-year teachers to develop the skills necessary for real two-way communication to take place. "Communication," defined as the verbal or nonverbal exchange of information, meaning, and feelings between two persons, covers every possible way we can interact. We may communicate well or poorly, but we cannot not communicate.

Parents need to feel that their concerns are important to teachers. When they feel "heard," they will be more enthusiastic about trusting the teacher and the school and working together on behalf of the child.

One of the most effective forms of communication with parents is "focused dialogue" (Hendricks 1988). It consists of three processes: mirroring, validation, and empathy.

Mirroring is the process of accurately reflecting back the content of a message from one person. The most common form of mirroring is "paraphrasing." A paraphrase is a statement in your own words of what the message sent means to you. Mirroring shows that you are willing to transcend your own thoughts and feelings for the moment and attempt to understand the other person's message. It permits you to paraphrase until you do understand (e.g., saying "You are really worried about your math grade," after a child sobbed "I failed my math test.")

Validation is a communication to the sending person that the information being received and mirrored "makes sense." Validation is a temporary suspension or transcendence of your point of view that allows the other person's experience to have its own reality. Typical validating phrases are: "I can see that..." "It makes sense to me that you would think that..." and "I can understand that...." Such phrases convey to the other person that the other person's message does not mean that you agree with his point of view or that it reflects your subjective experience. It merely recognizes the fact that in every situation, no "objective" view is possible. In any communication between two persons, there are always two points of view, and every report of any experience is an "interpretation" that is the "truth" for each person. The process of mirroring and validation affirms the other person's point of view and increases trust and closeness.

Empathy is the process of reflecting or imagining the feelings the sending person is experiencing about the event or the situation being reported. In this deep level of communication a person attempts to recognize, reach into, and, on some level, experience the emotions of the sending person.

Empathy allows both persons to transcend, perhaps for a moment, their separateness and to experience a genuine "meeting." Such an experience has remarkable healing power. Typical phrases for empathic communication include: "and I can imagine that you must feel...," "and when you experience that, I hear...understand you feel..." and "that makes sense."

Effective communication is essential to a good relationship because it gives the relationship meaning. Good communication skills may not solve problems or resolve issues, but no problems can be solved or issues resolved without them. According to Covey (1990), next to physical survival, the greatest need of a human being is psychological survival—to be understood, to be affirmed, to be validated, to be taken seriously, to be appreciated. Did you know that our communication consists of 10% words, 30% tone of voice (inflection), and 60% body language?

Teachers need to employ these communication skills whenever they have an opportunity to meet with parents. There are many formal and informal opportunities for meaningful dialogue. Two of the most popular forums for such encounters are open house and parent-teacher conferences. The following suggestions are made to help first-year teachers plan for these meetings with parents to ensure success.

III. THE OPEN HOUSE

An open house is another first impression for the beginning teacher. Other teachers can give you valuable advice. It is wise and useful to get the students involved in this event. Parents must feel welcomed and encouraged to become involved with their children's school and teachers.

PLANNING AN OPEN HOUSE

Follow these steps in planning an open house.

1. Send notes home well in advance to remind parents of "Open House."
2. Plan to have students' work on display and decorate the room.

3. Prepare a folder of the students' work to be placed on the desks. The parents can take the folder home.
4. Have a "Guest Book" for parents to sign.
5. Plan forms for obtaining parent volunteers for projects.
6. Plan an interesting way to introduce yourself to the parents.

CONDUCTING AN OPEN HOUSE

Schedule your time for the open house to include time to do the following:
1. Introduce yourself to the parents.
2. Provide a general overview of what the students will be learning this year.
3. Inform the parents of your management plan—the classroom rules, homework policy, grading system, and discipline plan.
4. Plan to distribute volunteer sign-up sheets at this time.
5. Schedule time for a few questions.
6. Refreshments can be provided in the room.
7. Ask your school administrator to announce over the intercom when it is time for the open house to be concluded.

Some parents will want to discuss their child individually. Be prepared to say something positive and if the parents want to schedule a conference, suggest that they indicate a convenient time on the form located on the table.

OPEN HOUSE "OPENERS"

You can prepare ahead of time ways to invite parents to the open house and ways to make them feel welcome in their child's classroom. Here are some ideas:
1. The children can make invitations to the "Open House."
2. One way to interest parents in coming to "Open House" is to take a video of each member of your class saying to his or her parent, "Gotcha!" Then have a contest to see how many of your students can persuade their parents to come to "Open House". When the parents get there, they will understand why it was so important to their child that they come—so they could see them on video.
OR
The teacher might prepare a video depicting the school day to be shown to

the parents. This is a project in which the students would be videotaped involved in the various activities of the day—including the academic subjects as well as special activities, lunch, and getting on and off the bus. This is an excellent way for parents to see what a day is like for their children as well as to see their children on video. (This also lets the teacher "off the hook" as far as having to stand in front of parents the whole night.)

3. Tape record the children reading and use that to begin the "Open House."

4. Get the children to make a life-size model of themselves and place them at their desks for "Open House." They can bring clothes from home, stuff them with paper and attach a paper plate head and feet which have been drawn by the student. The parent(s) love finding their child in the classroom and immediately know where they sit. They take the life-size model of their child home for the family to enjoy.

   OR

   Ask the student to bring in an old tee shirt that they will turn into a puppet representing themselves. The head can be made with a paper plate and the arms can be made from construction paper. With a coat hanger inside the shirt, the puppet can be attached to the student's chair to greet the parents. The shirt, with head and hands attached, can also be slipped over the back of the chair. Some students' hands could be raised and the child's work can be placed on the desks.

5. Make silhouettes of the children. Place them on the students' desks and let the parents locate "their child." The silhouettes make nice keepsakes.

6. Have the children leave notes on their desks for their parents and a sheet of paper for their parents to write a note back, which the children will get the following day.

7. Ask the children to finish these sentences about their parents:

   My mom laughs when......
   My father's favorite thing to do is......
   It makes me happy when my mother......

   Have the students place these sentences on their desks for their parents to read and enjoy.

8. Using the song "My Favorite Things" from The Sound of Music, children can write a list of their favorite things. The children write their names on the back of the list. The lists are hung around the room and parents try to identify their child's list.

9. Bring a squish ball to "Open House" with you. When it is time for introductions, tell one thing about yourself. Then throw the ball to a parent and ask him to do the same, adding the name of his child. The ball is thrown to another parent, who repeats this process. Do this until everyone in the room has been introduced.

IV. THE PARENT-TEACHER CONFERENCE

A parent-teacher conference is another opportunity to involve parents in the education of their children. Communication is vital in forming a partnership that works not only for the child but for the parent and teacher as well.

PLANNING A PARENT-TEACHER CONFERENCE

Follow these steps in planning a Parent-Teacher Conference:

1. Send a conference letter or form to the parents with a suggested time. Include spaces to acknowledge or suggest a better time to meet. Schedule conferences carefully. Try not to schedule too many conferences in one day. Allow a break time or schedule your name in some of the blocks to keep you on time. In order to keep from being rushed, plan a few conferences a week before and others the week after the official parent conference time. Include some times for working parents to attend.
2. Confirm the time.
3. Prepare a folder for each child. The folder should contain samples of student's work.
4. Plan an agenda for discussion.
5. Copy the conference schedule time (form) and jot down items to discuss.
6. Invite participation and support.
7. Conclude on a positive note.

CONDUCTING A CONFERENCE

Prepare in advance to include the following elements in your conference:

1. Place a few large "adult" chairs in the hall.

2. Post daily conference schedule on door.
3. Conduct conferences at a table in the back of the room away from the door. Again, include adult-size chairs. Keep notepaper and pencils handy so that you and/or the parents will be able to keep notes on the conference. (See Figure 14 for a sample form for parent conference notes and Figure 15 for a sample form for parent conference evaluation.)
4. Begin the conference with a friendly greeting. Plan to walk one parent to the door before inviting the next parent to come in.
5. Personalize the conference by sharing one positive experience, remark, or observation pertaining to their child.
6. Provide information in a straightforward and honest manner. Limit information to discuss. Focus on one or two important issues.
7. Be a listener and avoid interruptions. Respond in a precise and positive manner.
8. Provide suggestions for parents to work with their children. (See Figure 16 for ideas on building a child's self-esteem.)
9. Document the conference.

ETHICAL CONSIDERATIONS ● ● ● ● ● ● ● ● ● ● ● ● ● ● ● ● ● ● ●

There are a number of ethical considerations to think about before the conference:

1. Keep conference information confidential.
2. Avoid comparisons (e.g., this class with other classes or one student to other students or a student to his or her siblings).
3. Make no derogatory comments about the school, administration, principal, or faculty members.
4. Avoid confrontations.
5. Provide specifics and not generalities.
6. Remain neutral and objective; do not blame or pass judgments.

CONFERENCE IDEAS ●

Before the conference, prepare materials that will facilitate discussion with the parents. For example, you might:

1. Copy an article for parents that gives them suggestions on how to work with their child more effectively for school success.
2. Prepare a parent interest survey. Teachers might give parents a list of questions to be thinking about prior to the conference. For example, "What skills would

Figure 14. Sample Form for Parent Conference Notes

Parent Conference Notes

Student_____

Date _____

Attended by_____

Items We Discussed:

Evaluation of Conference:

Recommendations and Goals for the Future:

Specific Strategies to Try:

Teacher_____

Student_____

Parent_____

Figure 15. Sample Form for Parent Conference Evaluation

Parent Conference Notes

Would you please take a moment to evaluate our conference? Please review the rating scale and answer the questions by circling a number.

The Rating Scale	Excellent		Average		Poor
1. Rate the conference.	5	4	3	2	1
2. Was the conference helpful?	5	4	3	2	1
3. Rate the level of information shared.	5	4	3	2	1

If you have any suggestions or comments, please share them with me.

Figure 16. Ideas for Building a Child's Self-Esteem

1. Show your children that you like them by smiling at them, hugging them, and speaking to them in a positive way.
2. Read out loud together as a family.
3. Use positive reinforcement to encourage responsible behavior.
4. Help them to learn responsibility by requiring them to complete tasks.
5. Set aside a time each day to spend with each child individually.
6. Help children to develop organizational skills by providing space for toys, books, backpacks, and a place to work and/or study.
7. Help them to discover their own special gifts by letting them develop an interest in activities such as sports, music, and dance.
8. Encourage their independence.
9. Get to know their teachers.
10. Do not embarrass your children by yelling at them in public.
11. Try to help your child to achieve success in some way each day by offering a variety of activities.
12. Listen to your children and look them in the eyes when they are talking to you.
13. Do not set your expectations so high that the chance of failure prevents your child from trying.
14. Encourage your child to be proud of his or her name, ideas, and work. Pride makes a person try harder and strive to do better.
15. Give your child recognition for the effort he or she makes even though it may not come up to your expectations. If you do this, the child will continue to try.
16. Answer your child's questions openly, honestly, and immediately, if possible.
17. Take your child with you on trips to run errands and involve him or her in some of the decision making (e.g., "Should we go to the grocery store first or to Grandmother's first?")
18. Build a file of mementos of things in which your child participated.
19. Point out the unique qualities in your child (skills, attitudes, behaviors, abilities, desires, etc.) that make him or her special to you and others.
20. Do not compare one child to another.
21. Allow your children to express their feelings and let them know it's OK to do so.
22. Use a democratic form of discipline. Children should be allowed to talk and parents should listen to what they have to say.
23. Let your child know that you love him or her even when you disapprove of his or her behavior.
24. When discipline is necessary, do so with love. Discipline constructively, using positive suggestions, rather than destructively, using criticism.
25. Take time from work to eat lunch with your child or visit his or her school.
26. Let your child hear you praise him or her to other adults.
27. Welcome your children's friends into your home.

you like your child to learn?" or "Are you satisfied with your child's progress?"

Establishing a positive dialogue with parents is essential. When discussing the student, the teacher should provide good news first, then areas of needed improvement, and then return to more good news. For example:

> Teacher: "Johnny really loves math. I'm sure that is his favorite subject."
>
> Parent: "Yes, he's good in math."
>
> Teacher: "At times, he needs to be reminded to do his math homework. Do you have any ideas or suggestions that may help Johnny with his homework?"
>
> Parent: " I can check to see that his homework is finished."
>
> Teacher: " Johnny is given time to write his homework assignments in his notebook. I can check to see that he writes it in the notebook. Could you sign the notebook when he has completed his homework?"
>
> Parent: " Yes, I can go over his homework with him and sign his notebook each night."
>
> Teacher: " Thank you for your support. We want Johnny to be successful. I know we will have a great year."

Ribas (1992) offers several practical techniques that teachers can use to improve communication with parents:

> Be a good listener.
> Be positive.
> Be careful how you phrase negative information.
> Be prepared.
> Be sensitive to parents' problems.
> Be knowledgeable about the child as a person.

In addition, Ribas suggests that teachers call parents frequently, meet parents regularly, offer evening conference times, establish regular office or call-in hours, and send home a classroom newsletter.

3. Use a simple student interest survey as a conversation starter at parent-teacher conferences. (See Figures 17 and 18 for some sample interest surveys.) Place the sheet on top of the student's work you will be discussing, and share the results of the interest survey first. It is a good ice-breaker and demonstrates to the parents that you are interested in their child.

V. PARENT INVOLVEMENT IDEAS

Developing a partnership with the parent(s) is essential to the success of your classroom management plan. How can we work together to maximize students' learning potential? A letter can be sent home to initiate this partnership (see Parent Involvement Letter, Figure 19).

Many experienced teachers have contributed the following ideas that involve the parent(s). Before you read through this list, we suggest that you get a note pad and school calendar for each month. Without determination and careful planning, these ideas will stay on these pages and never get translated into practice.

✔ Send parents a questionnaire asking how they would like to be involved, what concerns they have about their child's education, and what special skills they might be willing to contribute to the learning process or to the classroom. (See Figure 20, Sample Parent Survey.)

✔ Plan monthly or seasonal special events when students invite their parents to share in activities that represent the culmination of a unit of study.

✔ Invite parents into the classroom to share their hobbies with the class (for example, crafts, coin collections, photography, stamp collections, sea shell collections, whittling, ham radio, sewing, or knitting).

✔ Send home a sign-up sheet for parents to volunteer to come in to read to the class (use one parent each week). This can be enjoyable for older students as well as younger ones, particularly if you help the parents in making the reading selections, and listen to their ideas.

✔ Schedule days when parents can come to school and walk through a day of school with their child. Plan this for one parent at a time, perhaps in conjunction with "Student of the Week" or "V.I.P." students.

✔ Find creative ways to involve parents in planning class parties—activities that are not too demanding of time and finances, but will make use of their own creativity. Support their ideas as much as possible.

✔ Have a parent lunch day where the children have earned the funds to

Figure 17. Sample Interest Survey

Interest Survey

What would you do if...

You were President of the United States?

You knew that you were going to be snowed in for a week?

You could invite one friend to go with you to Disney World? Who would you invite? Why?

You could trade lives with one person? Who would it be? Why?

You were given one million dollars?

You could have any job in the world?

You could change one thing about yourself?

Figure 18. Sample Interest Survey

Interest Survey

1. Which subject do you enjoy the most? Why?

2. I like the way I acted when...

3. I would like to work on...

4. I feel good about...

5. I enjoy school because...

Figure 19. Parent Involvement Letter

Dear Parents:

I'm writing to ask you to help me become a partner with you in your child's education. I know my teaching must begin with making your child feel at home in my classroom and with helping all the children come together in a learning community. Please help me get to know your child better by completing the following questions. Thank you for your time in sharing with me your thoughts about your child.

Sincerely,

Your child's name _____

What are your child's strengths? _____
_____
_____
_____
_____

What do you as a parent feel would be important for me to know?_____
_____
_____
_____
_____

What does your child enjoy doing?_____
_____
_____
_____
_____

Other comments _____
_____
_____
_____

Your name _____
Date _____

Figure 20. Sample Parent Survey

Parent Survey

Please complete this survey about your child and his or her interests. It will help me to become familiar with your child and assist with his or her needs.

_____

First   Middle   Last

Nickname_____

Address_____

Telephone _____

Birthdate _____

Allergies _____

Your child's favorite things to do _____
_____
_____
_____
_____

Your child's least favorite things to do_____
_____
_____
_____
_____

Things you would like to see your child achieve in school this year_____
_____
_____
_____
_____

Ways you would like to contribute to our class or our school this year (for example, reading books aloud to the class, computer tutoring, sharing cultural ideas, discussing what you do in your job, etc.)_____
_____
_____
_____

buy lunches for their parents.

✔ Look for ways to have parents bring in your "visual aids," such as a baby or toddler when you discuss human development, a grocery list, store advertisements and purchased groceries when you discuss money, math, or consumer practices, and favorite ethnic folktales or foods when you study other cultures.

✔ Have several parents come into the classroom at a time when you will be working on creative writing. You assign the topic and ask students to make their own rough drafts. Then assign a parent volunteer to each group of five students. Have the students read their stories aloud and invite the parents to help in editing.

✔ Have a parent type stories or poetry the class has written and make eye-catching displays.

✔ Involve parents in small group instruction. You may provide training sessions so that they will present correct information and instruction and teach according to your philosophy.

✔ Send activities home to a willing parent to cut, color, and paste for your centers or bulletin boards.

✔ Have parents come in to take slides or videotapes of class work and projects to be shown at the end of the year or at a movie party.

✔ Invite one parent weekly to bring ingredients and conduct a cooking activity using a favorite recipe. Have one or two parents compile the recipes at the end of the year to make a class cookbook for each child.

✔ Invite a parent to assist with teaching double Dutch (jump rope) to children who may not have learned this skill.

✔ Invite a parent to assist one group of students with work after you have worked with them (for example, the parent takes a reading group and helps to review and reinforce the skills while you work with another reading group).

✔ Invite parents to the classroom to discuss their jobs or professions.

✔ Have parents in the classroom as you teach a new skill or concept. During guided practice and independent practice, have parents monitor the work being done so that students are not completing assignments incorrectly.

✔ Invite a parent to be your newsletter editor. Encourage him or her to call on other parents for input.

✔ Parents can be invited to come into the classroom and relate their experience and life's joys with the children—becoming a significant other to the children simply by being there often to visit, talk, and listen to them.

✔ When you are working on any special projects, invite parents in to help. It's always nice to have extra hands for cutting, organizing, and distributing materials or answer questions.

✔ Have a parent who seems to have an interest and talent for developing center activities help you plan and create new ones each month.

✔ A parent could plan a spelling bee or facts contest or game.

✔ Ask a small group of parents to be in charge of a read-a-thon, math-a-thon, or some other contest.

✔ Make up and prepare simple skill games that can be sent home with the students. Older students may enjoy brain teasers and problem-solving situations. Games that encourage parent-child interaction will encourage parent-teacher interaction.

✔ Give an assignment asking parents to help their child write and/or draw pictures that would make up a short story. Plan a simple and nonthreatening competition with awards for best story, original plot, imaginative art, or funny story. You might hold the contest just for stories written and illustrated by the parents, letting the children select the winners.

✔ Give a regular weekly assignment that requires the parent to work with the child. If some parents are not responsive, find a school resource teacher who would be a "substitute parent" for such assignments so that the children feel special.

✔ Give students assignments that require them to ask questions of their parents.

✔ Ask parents to write an original poem, story, or brief report and bring it to share with the class. Have the parents show the students the various steps they took in writing the piece so that students can see that even adults have to go through a process to write and revise. Then display the finished product the parent has shared.

✔ Ask parents to clip pictures from magazines for your picture file (creative writing or center ideas).

✔ Ask parents to watch a particular television show with their child and discuss the show afterward.

✔ Ask parents to research upcoming television programming that may be of interest to the students or that follow your instructional topics and themes. Ask a parent to tape television programs for your class.

✔ Loan books, workbooks, and other materials to parents.

✔ Call parents on a regular basis to keep them informed on their child's progress, and to keep the communication lines open. Schedule some time to make a certain number of phone calls each Monday evening.

✔ Ask parents for information on their child's learning style and for their observations about how the child learns best.

✔ Schedule more parent-teacher conferences than you are required, or plan "office hours" when you are available at regular times for parents to call you or "walk in."

✔ Send home weekly progress reports. Design them to be interesting and something the parents look forward to receiving.

✔ Explain to parents certain techniques for teaching, for making learning materials, or for planning lessons. Invite parents to an actual inservice taught by you.

✔ Plan and design a monthly newsletter format that includes an introduction of each month's instructional plans and themes, as well as items that parents may be able to donate. Include scheduled blocks of time and specific events or duties for which parents can volunteer in the classroom. Add tips for parenting or items of interest and suggested reading for them and their children.

✔ Send thank you notes from you and notes from the students in appreciation of their support for your classroom.

✔ Applaud all parents with a standing ovation at every event they attend in the school or classroom.

✔ Give parents small incentives for every participation effort, such as award certificates, dollar-store "good mom" plaques, and so on.

✔ Offer a door prize, drawing, or some incentive for coming to an open house or other event in your classroom. Be sure to publicize it among all the families.

✔ Plan a continental breakfast for parents—early enough for them to come on their way to work.

✔ Invite parents to a lunch the children have planned and prepared, possibly ethnic food they have learned about through a study of other cultures.

✔ Plan special parent work days (with refreshments provided) where they help you with a special project.

✔ Hold monthly parent lunch days where parents eat lunch with their child in the classroom. Before the parents arrive, the students could decorate the tables with special tablecloths they made from art paper. Play soft music and make this a special event.

✔ Hold a video party for parents and students some evening after school. Show a video of a class activity and then a movie to enjoy. Provide popcorn and drinks.

✔ Hold a Saturday Family Activity where each parent would relate something positive about their family life. Display family albums, family projects, family trees, family recipes (and samples). Invite some of your friends to attend and take family snapshots or photographs. Call the event "Focus on Our Families."

✔ Hold a mini-workshop to teach parents and their child about book binding. Use cereal box front and back panels, and cover with contact paper. Encourage parents to help their children make books about family jokes, family trips, and other family events.

✔ Hold a multicultural fair and invite parents to come and be guest speakers, bring in food, or bring in arts and crafts. You may choose to have students be the guest speakers, cooks, and crafters, and invite the parents to attend the fair.

✔ Church groups sometimes will adopt a school, especially one in a low income area, and help in preplanned ways. If this is not already set up at your school, see if you can find a church auxiliary group that would be willing to adopt or sponsor your classroom. Their help could be in classroom aid, financial donations for materials for lower income students, or in crafting materials for your classroom.

Remember that the more parents are involved in the educational process, the better the chances are that their children will succeed in school. When students realize that their parents and teachers are working together on their behalf, they are more likely to commit the time and energy needed for academic excellence.

CHAPTER 4:

HOW CAN I SAVE TIME?

I. TIME MANAGEMENT

One of the advantages that seasoned teachers have is their ability to learn from their experiences. Most of them have figured out what is important and what can be skipped over or ignored. Most of them have also learned many shortcuts .

Our purpose for this chapter is to give you, the first-year teacher, the benefit of learning from seasoned teachers many of the "tricks of the trade." The chapter contains the many suggestions that they gave us to share with you. In every instance, they indicated that they wished someone had shared with them these ways to make teaching more enjoyable and their work more manageable.

We both conduct many workshops for teachers. At break time in one of those workshops, a teacher who had just completed his first year of teaching six classes of history at the secondary level asked for some advice. He admitted that he was overwhelmed and that his first year was not successful. Because the class was composed of experienced teachers, we suggested that we solicit ideas from them. It was difficult for the new teacher to discuss his concerns because he was afraid others would see them as weaknesses and him as a failure. To his surprise, the experienced teachers were very sympathetic and provided for him a wealth of information to make his second year less troublesome.

For example, one concern that he shared was that he was deluged with papers, reports, and projects to correct. He would go home with stacks—150 or more papers—to correct. One teacher asked if he made due dates the same for each class. He quickly said that he did. She commented that different due dates would allow him to correct fewer papers at one time. It was like a lightbulb had been turned on. It seemed like such a simple solution, but it was one that had not occurred to him.

Oftentimes, because they are so overwhelmed, first-year teachers fail to see ways to make things easier for themselves. The veteran teachers whom we have surveyed have been quite willing to share time management strategies that they have found to be useful—ways of cutting down or cutting out wasted time and energy. They know that the more of these they can implement, the more time they have left to be creative and productive and the less resentment they feel for the demands of their jobs.

We have called these strategies "Time Savers." We suggest that you read the ideas below with a magic marker in hand. Highlight the ideas that appeal to you.

II. TIME SAVERS

The following are suggestions that veteran teachers have shared with us for you.

✔ Each child has a pocket folder to take work back and forth from home. One side of the folder is used for school work and the other side is for newsletters, calendars, and messages. These folders can be laminated and slit at the pockets for more durability.

✔ I make student flip files for organizing and sorting student work and information. The materials needed for the files are: 1/2 of a file folder (the side with tab); a long strip of poster board (about one inch wider than the folders—12 1/2" x 18"; and clear tape. Position folders about one inch apart on poster board strip. Tape the edge of the folder half to the strip, taping on front and back. Place student name on the folder tab. Fifteen flip files on one strip of poster board would be the maximum one can hold.

✔ I have a great way to keep student papers in order and help students learn to be responsible for their work. Take a crate and put in hanging folders labeled with each students' name. In the folder are manila files labeled with subjects. When any work is done it is put in the folders. All work and tests are numbered. Then, when it is time to study for a test, I can tell the students to study 1-5 or 6, 7, and 10.

✔ I ask the children to sharpen pencils when they arrive at school in the morning before the bell rings. (They usually have 10-15 minutes between bus arrival and the morning bell.) When I don't want the pencil sharpener to be used (after the bell), I cover it with a sock. The children then know not to approach the sharpener, and not to ask. (I unplug the electric pencil sharpener.)

✔ I have "In/Out" pencil cans. Students may place a pencil that has a broken point or needs sharpening into the "in" can, and take a newly sharpened pencil from the "out" can to use. This saves time, assures the student of always having a sharpened pencil, and gives an opportunity for a student to sharpen all the pencils at a later designated time.

✔ In my classroom, each student has a clothespin with his or her name on it. I have a bulletin board with library pockets denoting different destinations, such as chorus, patrols, newspaper committees, bathroom, band, and so on. When students leave the room, they clip their clothespin to the appropriate pocket. This works well for me and cuts down on my having to rely on my memory.

✔ Whenever I decide to move students to another place in the room, instead of rearranging desks, I reassign them. This forces students to clear out their desks and make a clean start in another location.

✔ When the class needs a quick clean-up, play a game! Choose two students (volunteers or draw popsicle sticks) to stand back-to-back until you say "GO." Give the pair thirty seconds to pick up paper scraps, pencils, and/or crayons. After the thirty seconds has elapsed, the students compare who has the most items. The winner gets a sticker (or other treat). If there is still a need for additional clean-up, select two more students. Rule: Running causes immediate disqualification.

✔ Keep a small spray bottle of fingernail polish remover to use for wiping off lines from permanent markers from any laminated surface.

✔ So that I can quickly check attendance and lunch count, each child has a clothespin with his or her name on it. These are clipped on the "Absence Chart" (Figure 21) prior to the beginning of each day. This chart is placed by the door so that the students can move their clothespin to the "I'm buying lunch" section or the "I'm here today" section. I only need to glance at the chart to get attendance and the lunch count.

Figure 21. Absence Chart

I'm absent	I'm buying lunch	I'm here today

✔ My attendance plan is a simple system (see Figure 22). Instead of checking each person "present" or "absent" in the attendance book each day, I only fill in the date when the person is absent. If the student comes in late, I circle the date to indicate that he or she was only tardy. This makes it very easy to fill in the absentee/tardy section on report cards and student records, and saves me a lot of time.

Figure 22. Attendance Book System

John	5/17	(6/2)	6/5				
Susie							
Jack	(4/19)	6/2	6/3	6/4	6/5		

✔ After the first few weeks of school, when my classroom routine has settled down into a predictable pattern, I create a master form for each day and run off several copies. Since many regular events are different each day, but the same weekly, I need a separate master sheet for each day. I fill in the set schedule and basic information or instructions, and leave space for the specifics. This helps me write up my lessons plans quickly, and is invaluable to a substitute if I have to miss school unexpectedly.

✔ When recording grades in my grade book, I record test grades in RED, quiz grades in BLACK, and homework or class work grades in BLUE. This makes averaging grades easy when I do progress and grade reports. I automatically notice the test grades in RED and double them.

Figure 23. Grade Book System

John	90	98	100	100	( )	85
Susie	88	95	90	90	100	100
Jack	( )	89	94	99	100	100

To keep track of work needing to be collected from students who have been absent, I put a circle on the block where that grade belongs, and I can quickly find it to fill in that grade when the work is turned in (see Figure 23 for my grade book system).

✔ One of my favorite ideas to share is a way of arranging (and rearranging) students in the classroom. Prepare two sets of cards with, for example, multiplication facts, with problems on one set and the answers on the other set. As the students arrive for class (or at some other time), have them draw a card from a box or can. Then have them match their fact card to the correct answer card, which has been placed on a desk. This desk is their new seat. This activity reinforces their multiplication facts as well as adding a little fun to an old task.

Variations on the cards might include other skills such as: colors and their names; shapes and their names; numbers and the word form; animals and their names or habitats; states and their capitals.

✔ A successful technique I use in my classroom to save time is to assign each student a number. A student's number is determined by the alphabetical order in which the names are listed in my grade book, but when a new student arrives, he or she is just added to the end, receiving that number. Each time a student does an assignment, whether classwork or a test, he or she writes the number in the top right-hand corner of the paper. This system serves the following purposes:

1. The students can take turns filing papers in numerical order.
2. The children line up according to their numbers. I call numbers by groups of 5. For example, " 1 through 5 may line up."
3. I reward the group of 5 children that are the quietest in line. The children encourage the other members of their "fivesome" to cooperate and use soft voices during transitional times.
4. I put each child's number on a popsicle stick and select sticks at random to create cooperative learning groups.
5. I use the popsicle sticks to choose students to be special helpers, messengers, and game participants, and to select students for answering questions and building teams. It is a fair method to use because students are selected strictly by chance and it eliminates the likelihood of someone becoming a "teacher's pet." The "used" sticks remain out of the can until all have been chosen.
6. When I collect assignments, they are easily put in order, and if a

number is missing, I can tell immediately who has not turned in the work.

7. Sometimes I use individual mailboxes for paper distribution. The children know that the numbers also correspond with the mailboxes and are able to file for me both quickly and efficiently in their spare time.

There seem to be endless possibilities for this lottery-type number system, from choosing a line leader to choosing the student to say the Pledge of Allegiance at the open house or give morning announcements on the PA system with the principal. Parents find it democratic as well.

✔ Since I have two groups of students who come to my classroom and two children share the same desk, I laminate name tags with the name of the child from the morning class on one side and the name of the child from the afternoon class on the other. I put a piece of velcro stick tape on the corner of the desk and a piece on each side of the name tag. The children put their names on the desks when they enter the room. They place the name tag in the desk when they leave the room. I can see the names on the desks better and can take roll faster. Older students do not like name tags attached to them but enjoy name tags placed on their desks.

✔ Since communication with parents is such an important part of my teaching, I keep a record of parent contact. When sending notes home I use a carbon note pad (available commercially) and keep a copy on file. I also keep a record of phone conversations in a notebook. This helps me monitor parental contact as well as document conversations.

✔ For report card messages I have found useful examples in a book by McDonald and Lake (1971).

✔ I begin each school day with journal time. As the children enter, after unpacking, they are expected to write in their journals. Soft music makes this a relaxed and enjoyable time. This starts the day quietly and reflectively, and helps the students have an opportunity to express some unresolved feelings they may have experienced at home or on the way to school. I like to follow this time with a sharing time and a planning time with the class.

✔ I am known as the "sticker lady" in my classroom. I always have my pockets filled with stickers. Many times when I see children who are obeying the rules, I place a sticker on them and verbalize what I like about what they are doing. This makes the other children take notice and mimic the rewarded behavior. This is especially helpful when establishing new behaviors.

✔ I make (laminate) several large yellow buses for my room and then place a number on the side of each bus. I cut out people and write on them the names of the students who are riding that bus. Above the buses, I write "Bus Business."

✔ I put tennis balls on the legs of the chairs to keep the noise down and add color and fun to the room. They are slit and placed on the chair legs. Old tennis balls can be provided by the students or parents.

✔ One of the projects that I have used in my sixth grade classroom to help students gain a sense of responsibility is to set aside time for them to work with kindergarten students. Some of the activities include: writing stories that the kindergarten students dictate, reading to the students, and playing educational games dealing with numbers and letters.

✔ My first graders were very rowdy every day after lunch. I asked the teacher of a third grade class if one student could come each day to my classroom to read when we returned from lunch. The third graders had to take the book home and practice reading at night so that they would be prepared. We chose the Boxcar Children series, by Gertrude Chandler Warner, to read.

My children started returning eagerly from lunch. They put their lunch boxes away quickly and sat down on the rug to listen to the reader of the day. The third grade teacher reported that oral reading skills improved and that even the most timid students in the classroom began to ask for a turn to read. My students made bookmarks for the third grade classroom and gave them awards for being "Reading Friends."

✔ I use lots of student interest surveys, for example, when conferencing with students or talking with parents. I also include them in the student portfolios. The information I learn from the surveys is very useful for planning units and activities and for goal setting. I can personalize the curriculum to the needs and interests of the students.

✔ I send home a Teacher's Report Card (Figure 24), which helps me in planning for the following year and lets the parents know I am concerned about my performance and self-improvement. This form can be modified and completed by students as well.

✔ I like to send weekly reports home to let the parents see their child's progress. This is not too much of a hassle if you find or design a simple form to use (see Figure 25 for a sample reading log).

✔ When the whole class is interacting or talking, raise your hand.

Figure 24. Teacher's Report Card

Teacher's Report Card

Dear Parents,

Please take a few minutes to complete this report card. Thank you for your assessment.

Grading Scale

A = Excellent   B = Good

C = Average   NI = Needs Improvement

1. Did your child learn a lot of valuable information?
   A _____
   B _____
   C _____
   NI _____

2. Did your child get more interested in his/her learning?
   A _____
   B _____
   C _____
   NI _____

3. Did your child enjoy school more this year?
   A _____
   B _____
   C _____
   NI _____

4. How do you feel about the amount of homework assigned?
   A _____
   B _____
   C _____
   NI _____

5. Indicate an overall teaching grade.
   A _____
   B _____
   C _____
   NI _____

Comments:

Figure 25. Sample Reading Log

My Reading Log

Books Completed	Started	Finished	Comments

When the children see your hand, they raise their hands and get quiet. This spreads around the classroom very quickly. The best part is that you don't have to say a word or lose patience. When your hand goes down, the class should remain silent until further directions. This should be presented as a game. It's important to use this in a positive manner, praising the students who raise their hands first.

✔ One attention-getting device I use if the children are not following directions is to whisper something positive in the ear of one or two children who I find are listening. For example, I might just walk over and whisper, "Sally, I like the way you are standing quietly waiting for the next set of instructions," or I might whisper, "Thanks, Billy, for holding on to the ball and not bouncing it." The other children stop what they are doing because they want to hear what I whispered to the others.

✔ While standing in line waiting for the buses to be called, we sing and draw shapes in the air, sing vowel jingles, and count by 5's and 10's.

✔ I clap a rhythm to get the children's attention. They clap the rhythm back to me. I continue doing this until all children are quiet and paying attention. Changing the rhythm makes it more interesting.

✔ One effective behavioral management technique I use is earning marbles. This method involves positive reinforcement of the whole class. When everyone is following the class rules, they will be rewarded by having a marble transferred from one jar to another.

This behavioral technique has several successive steps. The first step is to earn ten marbles. I have two jars on my desk in front of the room. One jar is empty. The other jar is filled with marbles. When I see the whole class following the rules, I reward them by taking a marble out of the full jar and dropping it into the empty jar. I reward their good behavior often and we quickly earn the ten marbles. When the tenth marble has been earned, we stop whatever it is we are doing and either go outside or stay inside and have free time. A marble earned cannot be taken away.

After the students have earned the ten marbles, they are put back into the first jar and we start again. This time they must earn thirty marbles. When they do, we stop and have free time.

The third step is to have all the marbles from one jar transferred to the other jar. When the last marble has been dropped into the jar, we stop what we are doing and choose a "big treat"—a snack and a movie, drawing, reading, or playing games.

✔ Sometimes I find it necessary to offer visual reminders of behavior agreements. Behavior contracts (see Figures 26 and 27, sample behavior contracts) work well because they remind students that their behavior is their choice.

✔ Each month, I reserve half of a bulletin board for my candy calendar. I attach seasonal candies to the calendar, one for each school day of the week. Small stickers, which represent free homework passes, are hidden behind six of the candies. At the end of the day, a drawing is held to see who wins the candy. To be eligible for the drawing, students must have displayed good behavior during the day, completed all assignments, and obeyed class rules. (They can keep their own points during the day—and I announce how many points they must have to be eligible for the drawing.) A different person draws each day, but only when everyone is seated and ready to go home. The candy calendar really makes for a quick, quiet dismissal. And my students never let me forget it!

✔ In my classroom, I use a "class meeting" technique. If there is a problem with one child hurting another or fighting in my class, a student can call us together to problem-solve how to handle the situation. I can also call a class meeting.

Figure 26. Sample Behavior Contract

I will remember not to forget my contract

For:_____

I will be in my seat when the bell rings—for 5 consecutive days.

_____ (student) will help to remind me.

My teacher will help by saying "I like the way _____ is in (his or her) seat before the bell rings."

To celebrate, I will be able to be line leader for 5 consecutive days.

Date _____

Helper _____

Teacher _____

Figure 27. Sample Behavior Contract

Work Contract

I'm jumping in to say

When: I can recite the multiplication tables for 6 and 7

Then: I can get a homework pass

Date_____

My name_____

Teacher's name_____

Contract reviewed on (date) _____

When we are together on the rug, I ask the child who called the meeting to explain the problem as he or she saw it. After all sides have had a chance to explain and/or defend themselves, the children help me decide whether or not there should be consequences.

The children are usually very fair and listen to their peers. The consequences range from missing ten minutes of free time to writing an apology note to the hurt friend.

III. REFLECTIVE TEACHING

Reflecting on one's teaching provides an opportunity to evaluate, rethink, and chart a new course of action in achieving goals while saving time. The majority of the first-year teachers we surveyed knew they needed time to reflect on teaching but were unable to find the time. One teacher said, "Reflecting is nice, but who has time for nice?"

An experienced teacher was asked to comment on that statement and said, "Reflecting is wise; being wise saves time." Experienced teachers reflect on their teaching constantly in order to improve efficiency, maintain consistency, and reduce wasted time.

In order to be wise, first-year teachers need to learn to reflect systematically on their teaching. They need to constantly ask themselves, "What is working?" "What is not working?" and What is another way?"

Three important words on which first-year teachers need to concentrate are REFLECT, REGROUP, and RETURN. Many teachers ask, " How do I find the time to reflect?" In order to find the time, it must be a top priority. Call it "My Time." Mark a place for it in the plan book and condition yourself to routinely use this time for yourself. You will find that by establishing this habit and sticking to it, you will begin to feel its importance in helping you to feel "on top of" your teaching situation (instead of living with the fear that it is "on top of" you).

Other teachers have suggested that another way to reflect on one's teaching is to keep a teaching log or journal. The teacher can set aside ten minutes of "Journal Time" each day as the children write in their journals. The format of a daily teaching log or journal might be as follows: (1) write a positive observation, (2) report an area of need, (3) develop two strategies that meet that need, and (4) identify a key word for the next day. If writing in the teaching log or journal every day feels like a burden, it might be wise to establish one day a week to devote to this practice. For instance, you could designate Thursday immediately after school as your uninterrupted "Journal Time" (see Figure 28 for a sample Weekly Observation Form, which may help you in your reflection). Another format for a

Figure 28. Weekly Observation Form

Weekly Observations

Name _____

Date _____

Name three things that you feel good about that you did this week.

_____

_____

_____

Name one time when you stopped yourself from making a mistake.

_____

_____

_____

Name one thing you would like to do next week that you haven't tried before. _____

_____

_____

What was your favorite activity this week: _____

_____

_____

_____

Who helped and encouraged you the most during the past week? _____

_____

Describe the learning experience. _____

_____

_____

_____

Who was the person you helped and encouraged the most this past week?

_____

Describe the learning experience. _____

_____

_____

_____

weekly journal or teaching log might be as follows: (1) write one thing you liked about the week, (2) identify one area that needs improvement, and (3) develop two strategies you plan to implement on Monday.

Another suggestion offered by veteran teachers was to join a support group. Some mentioned a formal group that met one afternoon or evening each week; others said that going out together on Friday afternoons met this need. Still others set up a computer network with four or five teachers with whom they communicated each week at a designated time. This time together became very important, as it provided a way to get feedback and suggestions, as well as an opportunity to express frustrations and needs with others who were having similar experiences.

The truth remains, however, that it is the teacher who must not only know and enjoy the subject matter, but who must know and enjoy his or her students and find ways to manage time and energy so as to maximize learning and efficiency in the classroom.

All in all, the success of one's first year of teaching lies in the attitude of the teacher. If the teacher feels successful, he or she will, in all likelihood, be successful. This is not to say that the teacher won't make mistakes, but it is to say that he or she will take each mistake as an opportunity to learn and grow. As the year unfolds, hopefully he or she will begin to feel the excitement of challenging young minds and seeing children turned on to their ability to learn and master, seek and find, accomplish and succeed.

As Emerson once said, "That which we persist in doing becomes easier—not that the nature of the task has changed, but our ability to do has increased." (Covey 1990, 318). Hopefully, this book has provided you, the first-year teacher, with the tools you need to help you to feel effective, creative, useful, and productive. Our hope is that, with its help, you will have found your first year of teaching to have been both worthwhile and fulfilling. We also hope that, with it behind you, you will be excitedly looking forward to embarking on another adventure— your second year of teaching—knowing that it too will be a time when you will have an opportunity to change lives and plant seeds in the generation that will live on after you are gone.

CHAPTER 5:

HOW DO I END THE YEAR?

I. TEACHER AS A PROFESSIONAL

Many times, we hear a teacher described as "just" a teacher. We need to do our part to raise the status of the teacher, not just in the eyes of the community, but in our own eyes as well.

To begin, teachers must see themselves as professionals. Their students must be seen as clients. The "practice of teaching" involves meeting needs and satisfying our students. This process starts in the first year. The beginning year is critical in establishing positive relationships with school administrators, faculty, students, and parents.

As one second-year teacher commented,

> You have earned a degree and your opinion and decisions are of value. Don't be intimidated.

Another veteran teacher offered this advice:

> Act confidently (even if you're scared). Remember teachers with years of experience are unsure at the beginning of each school year.

The following are suggestions that experienced teachers have shared with us:

✔ Form a peer group to act as a support group for the first year and meet regularly.
✔ Keep in touch with friends, colleagues, and university professors.

✔ Keep a journal.

✔ Set personal and professional goals for the first teaching year.

✔ Join a health spa or develop an exercise program. Never sacrifice this time, for it is necessary to replenish an exhausted body and mind.

✔ Eat healthy foods and get plenty of sleep.

✔ Tape several songs that you enjoy hearing or singing. Listen to them in the car on the way to work.

✔ Check out audiotapes and listen to them before or after school.

✔ Smile, stay positive, idealistic, and continue to believe in yourself. You must become your own advocate.

✔ Subscribe to professional journals and attend professional conferences. Join professional organizations.

✔ Read books for pleasure as well as keeping up with the latest trends in your profession.

II. COUNT DOWN: THE LAST MONTH

The end of the year requires as much planning as the beginning of the year. Everyone is tired. Time is running out. The paperwork demands are extreme; the students are ready to go, but a few weeks remain. Plan some special events that may include storytellers; speakers; persons from the city or community to discuss summer activities, water safety, or projects for volunteers; a local news team to discuss news, production, and reporting; and local people to discuss student-selected topics of interest.

Rewards, recognitions, and "catch them being good" must still be an active part of classroom management. Individual and group goals and rewards are necessary to keep the students actively engaged in the learning process to the very end. Use student input to direct the selection of the final two-week plan of study.

Remember that the last days are hectic. Often books have been collected and the students are without textbooks for these last days. Sometimes special classes such as music, art, physical education, and library are stopped one to two weeks before school ends. This means that the students are with you more of the time. It is important to continue with the same management plan of operation, routines, and procedures.

• •

Several veteran classroom teachers have suggested the following ideas to sustain students' interest and enthusiasm in school during the final weeks or days.

In preparing these end-of-the-year Learning Units, start about three to four weeks prior to the end of school. Use the same lesson plan outline form (see Figure 3) and the same management plan format described in chapter 2.

Individual Work Projects

• •

1. **Independent Review Packets.** Students complete dittoed review sheets for one or more subjects.
2. **Independent "Learning Unit" (ILU)**. (See the following example.)
   Topic: Seven U.S. Regions

   Each student receives a file folder with a blank U.S. map stapled to the inside. The student decorates the folder cover to depict the contents of the folder. Each folder contains a cover sheet with a list of activities to be completed in a week. On Monday, the unit is introduced; Tuesday and Wednesday, students work independently; Thursday, the folder is checked; and Friday, a quiz is given. Students can work on units any time, such as before and after assemblies or when the teacher needs to work on end-of-year checklist procedures.

   The following activities might be included in the file folders:

   a Locate and label states and their capitals on your U.S. map.
   b. Describe each area.
   c. Locate rivers and mountain ranges.
   d. Choose a state, cite interesting facts, and describe its importance.
   e. Draw a poster advertising an area.
   f. Complete chapter questions or worksheets.
   g. Categorize items about the region.
   h. Make graphs of the area statistics.
   i. Prepare oral presentations.

Group Work Projects

• •

1. **Create Books for the Class Library (writing, illustrating, and binding).** The teacher will need to get parents to help and a librarian or resource

teacher to demonstrate book making. Guest speakers during the unit may be authors, illustrators, and publishers. Students work in pairs or groups. Students can read their books to other classes.

2. **Design Study Guides for New Students.** This activity is a good review of the curriculum. Cooperative learning groups may be formed and each group assigned a subject. Put all the information together into a study guide for new students.

3. **Develop a Booklet or Pamphlet: "Everything you Need to Know About Sixth Grade to Survive and Be Successful."** (This can be developed for any grade level.) Use cooperative learning groups to develop text. Assign tasks within the group to design booklet, compile information, illustrate, and bind the booklet. Students can share booklets or pamphlets with each other or other classes.

4. **Write an End-of-the-Year Newsletter.** This idea has already been developed in the 30-day management plan (see Chapter 2). This particular end-of-the-year edition could include subject reviews, class overviews, changes for next year, awards, assemblies, recognition information, interviews with first-year teachers, advice for next year, and student plans for the summer.

Resource people may be invited to the class, for example, local newspaper writers and editors, to provide ideas, assistance, and hints. They might give your class or school some exciting press coverage. Some good end-of-the-year school news can only help.

Integrated Review Projects

Teacher(s) select a topic and plan instruction, review sheets, activities, puzzles, games, or mind benders to be completed for each subject matter area. A culminating event or activity would enhance the unit.

1. **Create Time Capsules.** Time capsules are designed by each student to contain memorabilia of the school year—such as headlines depicting interesting, noteworthy events, items of interest, review sheets of the curriculum, and advice or success. The container itself must be designed by the student. When the time capsule is completed, the student can bury or hide it. The student then draws a map leading to the capsule and gives it to the teacher for the next years' students to enjoy.

2. **Teach a Lesson.** Students choose their favorite subject and plan and teach a lesson to the class. This will give them an opportunity to be creative and innovative and will keep students engaged in learning activities even at the end of the year. Other project ideas are as follows:

1. Have your students read stories to kindergartners or first graders.
2. Plan cross-age tutor-partner time.
3. Have students pick a topic or hobby and share it with the class in a creative way.
4. Have students report on their favorite book and compile a class list entitled "Most Wanted Books." The list can also include a summary and a line or two for rating the reading/book (similar to the movie ratings).

III. END-OF-THE-YEAR MANAGEMENT PLAN

THE LAST THREE WEEKS
GOAL: END THE YEAR WITH CONFIDENCE

Key Teaching Areas:
❑ Continue to teach management plan.
❑ Maintain routines, cues, and procedures.
❑ Introduce Learning Units.
❑ Discuss expectations.

Strategies for Success:
❑ Prepare students for Learning Units.
❑ Intersperse introduction of Learning Units within daily schedule.
❑ Present resource material and/or people.

With three weeks of school remaining, use Week 1 to prepare students for selecting learning units for the end-of-year activities. Use Weeks 2 and 3 to teach the selected units. The following is a plan for the five days of Week 1.

DAY 1—PLAN FOR SUCCESS

BEGIN THE DAY: Teacher and student greeter meet the students in the morning.

ROUTINE PROCEDURE: The routine procedure every morning is for the students to first get prepared for class upon entering the room and then to write in their journals for ten minutes.

OPENING ACTIVITY: Ask students to word web what they would like to learn in the remaining weeks of school. Explain that suggestions must be realistic but creative, different, and fun. List the suggestions on the chalkboard under the heading, "Ideas for Learning." The teacher can add a few to the list. Discuss the ideas and learning opportunities. Students can then reduce the list and select several ideas. Put students into Think, Pair, Share teams or groups to begin developing ideas. Share ideas and collect their ideas.

USE CUE: Raise your hand and move to the front of the room to get the students' attention. You may need, once again, to monitor the amount of time it takes to get everyone's attention. If students take too much time, take time from students to reinforce this procedure.

ACTIVITY: Continue with scheduled curriculum lesson plans.

AFTER-LUNCH ROUTINE: Specialized time for preparing the students for the end of the year and the Learning Units. This may be scheduled time for additional preparation or planning of the Learning Units.

ACTIVITY: Continue with lesson plans.

END-OF-THE-DAY ROUTINE: Closure—Read the selected "Ideas for Learning." Suggest that students bring in more ideas for the Learning Units.

REMINDERS:
   ✔ Remember "Marble Jar" for group rewards.

DAY 2—TEACH THAT "EFFORT EQUALS OUTCOME" ● ● ● ● ● ● ●

BEGIN THE DAY: Teacher and student greeter meet the students in the morning.

ROUTINE PROCEDURE: The routine procedure every morning is for the students to first get prepared for class upon entering the room and then to write in their journals for ten minutes.

OPENING ACTIVITY: Ask students for additional suggestions they've come up with for the Learning Unit. Record them on a list that you are keeping to plan the Learning Units.

USE CUE: Raise your hand and move to the front of the room to get the students' attention.

ACTIVITY: Continue with scheduled curriculum lesson plans.

AFTER-LUNCH ROUTINE: Specialized time for preparing the students for the end of the year and the Learning Unit. Provide specific information or materials.

ACTIVITY: Continue with curriculum lesson plans.

END-OF-THE-DAY ROUTINE: Say to students: "Tell me one thing you learned today? Tell me one thing you relearned today? Tell me one thing you will enjoy about the Learning Units?"

REMINDERS:
   ✔ Plan and prepare Learning Units.
   ✔ Need file folders.

DAY 3—LEARNING CAN BE FUN

BEGIN THE DAY: Teacher and student greeter meet the students in the morning.

ROUTINE PROCEDURE: The routine procedure every morning is for the students to first get prepared for class upon entering the room and then to write in their journals about the Learning Units.

OPENING ACTIVITY: Students share ideas about possible learning units. The teacher can list them on the chalkboard. The students vote on the learning units they would like for the remaining two weeks of class. Discuss whether this is a realistic number of learning units. Have they selected too many? Review selections and vote again. Majority rules and the Learning Units have been selected by the class. Teacher lists them on the front board.

USE CUE: Raise your hand and move to the front of the room to get the students' attention. You may need, once again, to monitor the amount of time it takes to get everyone's attention. If students take too much time, take time from students to reinforce this procedure.

GUIDELINES: Review the "Guidelines for Giving Directions." The students will be working in committees, cooperative learning groups, or pairs during the Learning Units and this procedure needs to be reinforced. Set up two scenarios of this procedure and ask students what step is missing. Ask why procedures are important to the success of the Learning Units.

ACTIVITY: Continue with scheduled lesson plans.

AFTER-LUNCH ROUTINE: Specialized time for preparing the students for the end of the year and the Learning Units. This may be scheduled time for additional preparation or planning of the "Learning Units." Resource people may come in to share information or demonstrate such learning activities. You can collect support information to share at this time or students may begin to read books pertaining to the topics.

ACTIVITY: Continue with curriculum lesson plans.

END-OF-THE-DAY ROUTINE: Closure—How can you contribute to the success of the Learning Units? What are some ideas that may be helpful?

REMINDERS:
  ✔ Catch Them Being Good!
  ✔ Pass out candy treats.

DAY 4—PLAN FOR THE END OF THE YEAR AS IF IT WERE THE BEGINNING

BEGIN THE DAY: Teacher and student greeter meet the students in the morning.

ROUTINE PROCEDURE: The routine procedure every morning is for the students to first get prepared for class upon entering the room and then to write in their journals for ten minutes. Pick a topic related to the selected Learning Units.

OPENING ACTIVITY: Students brainstorm ideas pertaining to the selected Learning Units. Take each Learning Unit and do a word web of ideas. Students copy the webs to refer to later. At this time, students may need to be assigned to cooperative learning groups or committees for specific work assignments.

USE CUE: Raise your hand and move to the front of the room to get the students' attention.

GUIDELINES: The teacher reviews "LEAP into Learning Together" rules. The students will be working and learning together during the Learning Units and these rules (expectations) for group interaction need to be discussed, modeled, and reinforced.

ACTIVITY: Continue with scheduled curriculum lesson plans.

AFTER-LUNCH ROUTINE: This may be scheduled time for students to plan the Learning Units.

ACTIVITY: Continue with curriculum lesson plans.

END-OF-THE-DAY ROUTINE: Ask students: Why are we practicing "LEAP into Learning Together" with the Learning Units?

REMINDERS:
- ✔ Set up a calendar or schedule to organize the Learning Unit.
- ✔ Make copies of "Guidelines for Giving Directions" and "LEAP into Learning Together" rules for groups to place in the file folders.
- ✔ Prepare an agenda sheet. See Day 5 under OPENING ACTIVITY.

DAY 5—END WITH DIGNITY

On the Friday before the unit begins on Monday, ready the students and introduce the selected Learning Units that they will have two weeks to complete.

BEGIN THE DAY: Teacher and student greeter meet the students in the morning.

ROUTINE PROCEDURE: The routine procedure every morning is for the students to first get prepared for class upon entering the room and then to write in their journals for ten minutes.

OPENING ACTIVITY: Pass out the file folder to plan the Learning Unit. Pass out and discuss the calendar or schedule for students to record working time for the Learning Unit. Develop time lines for the assignments and activities. Place the calendar or schedule in each Learning Unit file folder and collect. Place the folder for student access and return it to the same location each day. You may want to design an agenda sheet for the students to complete each day to summarize what was done, note progress, note where they left off, and establish plans for the next day. All materials stay in the folder. Students may need to bring in a box to keep information, supplies, and materials.

USE CUE: Raise your hand and move to the front of the room to get the students' attention.

ACTIVITY: Continue with scheduled curriculum lesson plans.

AFTER-LUNCH ROUTINE: Read aloud to students or provide time for Sustained Silent Reading (SSR).

ACTIVITY: Continue with curriculum lesson plans.

END-OF-THE-DAY ROUTINE: Ask students: "What are Learning Units? When do we start? How do we learn together? What is the product?"

REMINDERS:
    ✔ Make a progress sheet to staple inside the cover of file folder.

For the next two weeks, the teacher will be teaching the selected Learning Units. In Week 3 (the last week of school) students will make class presentations of their Learning Units. Parents may be invited to attend the presentations.
    Planning for the end of the school year can reduce the deterioration of academic performance and bring a strong sense of closure to the first year of teaching (Merrill 1991).

• •

Beginning teachers suffer alone through numerous problems and operate under a considerable amount of stress, anxiety, and unrealistic self-imposed expectations. Many first-year teachers cope with the most difficult students, take on time-consuming extracurricular activities, and are named to several school committees. The first year is a year that remains in our memory forever.
    The authors are interested in your comments, suggestions, and ideas that may be included in the next edition of this book. Please forward your comments to us at this address: Dr. Karen Bosch, Virginia Wesleyan College, Norfolk, Virginia 23502-5599 and Dr. Katharine Kersey, Old Dominion University, Norfolk, Virginia 23529-3260. As always, we wish you the best teaching years ever!

BIBLIOGRAPHY

Anderson, L. 1989. *The Effective Teacher.* New York: Random House.

Arends, R. 1991. *Learning to Teach.* New York: McGraw-Hill.

Berla, N. 1992. "Getting Middle School Parents Involved." *Education Digest* 58, no. 2:18-19.

Bloom, B. S., ed. 1956. *Taxonomy of Educational Objectives, Handbook I: Cognitive Domain.* New York: David McKay.

Bosch, K. A. 1991. "Cooperative Learning: Instruction and Procedures to Assist Middle School Teachers." *Middle School Journal 22,* no. 3:34-35.

Bosch, K. A. and Kersey, K. C. 1993. "Just Be Quiet and Learn." *Clearing House* 66, no. 4:229.

Brooks, D. M. 1985. "The First Day of School." *Educational Leadership* 42, no. 8:76–78.

Bullough, R. 1989. *First-Year Teacher: A Case Study.* New York: Teachers College, Columbia University.

Charles, C. M. 1992. *Building Classroom Discipline.* New York: Longman.

Clark, C. and Elmore, J. 1979. *Teacher Planning in the First Weeks of School.* Research series no. 56. East Lansing, Michigan: Institute for Research on Teaching, Michigan State University.

Covey, S. R. 1990. *The 7 Habits of Highly Effective People.* New York: Simon & Schuster.

Drayer, A. 1979. *Problems in Middle and High School Teaching.* Boston: Allyn and Bacon.

Emmer, E. T., Evertson, C. M. and Anderson, L. M. 1980. "Effective Classroom Management at the Beginning of the School Year." *Elementary School Journal* 80:219-231.

Evertson, C. M. and Anderson, L. M. 1979. "Beginning School." *Educational Horizons* 57:164-168.

Evertson, C. M. and Emmer, E. T. 1982. "Effective Management at the Beginning of the School Year in Junior High Classes." *Journal of Educational Psychology* 74:485-498.

Evertson, C. M. 1989. "Improving Elementary Classroom Management: A School-based Training Program for Beginning the Year." *Journal of Educational Research* 83, no. 2:82-90.

Good, T. L. and Brophy, J. 1987. *Looking in Classrooms,* 4th ed., New York: McGraw-Hill.

Henderson, A. 1987. *The Evidence Continues to Grow: Parent Involvement Improves Student Achievement.* Columbia, Md.: National Committee for Citizens in Education.

Hendricks, H. 1988. *Getting the Love You Want.* New York: Harper & Row.

Huling-Austin, L., Odell, S., Ishler, P., Kay, R. and Edelfelt, R. 1989. *Assisting the Beginning Teacher.* Reston, Va.: Association of Teacher Educators.

Hunter, M. 1989. "Join the 'Par-aide' in Education." *Educational Leadership* 47, no. 2:36-39.

Jennings, W. 1989. "How to Organize Successful Parent Advisory Committees." *Educational Leadership* 47, no. 2:42-45.

Jones, V. and Jones L. 1990. *Comprehensive Classroom Management.* Boston: Allyn & Bacon.

Kane, P. R., ed. 1991. *The First Year of Teaching.* New York: Penguin Books.

Kersey, K. C. 1990. *Don't Take It Out On Your Kids.* Washington, D.C.: Acropolis Books, Ltd., 1990.

Knowles, J. 1990. "Understanding Teaching Perspectives." *Journal of Teacher Education* 41, no. 1:28-38.

Krajewski, R. J. and Shuman, R. B. 1979. *The Beginning Teacher: A Practical Guide to Problem Solving.* Washington, D.C.: National Education Association.

McDonald, M. and Lake, D. 1971. *Teachers' Messages for Report Cards.* Belmont Calif.: Fearon Teacher Aid Book.

Merrill, A. 1991. "Planning for the End of the Year at a Middle School." *Middle School Journal* 22, no. 5:5-9.

Moran, S. W. 1990. "Schools and the Beginning Teacher." *Phi Delta Kappan* 72, no. 3:210-213.

Ribas, W. B. 1992. "Helping Teachers Communicate with Parents." *The Principal* 72, no. 2:19-20.

Ryan, K., ed. 1970. *Don't Smile Until Christmas.* Chicago: University of Chicago Press.

Ryan, K., ed. 1986. *The Induction of New Teachers.* Bloomington, Ind.: Phi Delta Kappa Educational Foundation.

Sachar, E. 1991. *Shut Up and Let the Lady Teach.* New York: Poseidon Press.

Schell, L. M. and Burden, P. 1992. *Countdown to the First Day of School.* Washington, D.C.: NEA Professional Library.

Smith, M. M. 1993. "The Beginning Teacher's First Month." *Kappa Delta Pi Record* 29, no. 4:120-125.

Strother, D. 1985. "Practical Applications of Research: Classroom Management." *Phi Delta Kappan* 66, no. 10:723-728.

Tonnsen, S. and Patterson, S. 1992. "Fighting First-year Jitters." *The Executive Educator* 14, no. 1:29-30.